Illustrator:
Howard Chaney

Editor:
Walter Kelly, M.A.

Editor in Chief:
Sharon Coan, M.S. Ed.

Creative Director:
Elayne Roberts

Art Coordination Assistant:
Cheri Macoubrie Wilson

Cover Art:
Denise Bauer

Imaging:
Ralph Olmedo, Jr.

Production Manager:
Phil Garcia

Publishers:
Rachelle Cracchiolo, M.S. Ed.
Mary Dupuy Smith, M.S. Ed.

EXPLORING MARS AND BEYOND
Challenging

Written by Greg Young, M.S. Ed.

Teacher Created Materials, Inc.
6421 Industry Way
Westminster, CA 92683
©1998 Teacher Created Materials, Inc.
Made in the U. S. A.
ISBN-1-57690-383-4

The classroom teacher may reproduce copies of materials in this book for classroom use only. The reproduction of any part for an entire school or school system is strictly prohibited. No part of this publication may be transmitted, stored, or recorded in any form without written permission from the publisher.

Table of Contents

Introduction 3

Early Space Exploration

   Birth of Space Exploration 4
   Important Events: 1926–1969 5
   Robert Goddard and Wernher von Braun 6
   Goddard and von Braun—Check for Understanding 7
   Activity #1: Air-Powered Rocket Launch 8
   Activity #2: Liquid-Powered Rocket Launch 10
   Sputnik and *Explorer* 12
   Activity #3: Newton's Third Law 13
   Luna and *Ranger* 14
   Searching for Astronauts 15
   Vostok and *Mercury* 16
   Activity #4: Egg Drop 17
   Voskhod and *Gemini* 19
   Venera and *Mariner* 20
   Surveyor and *Zond* 21
   Apollo and *Soyuz* 22
   Space Race—Check for Understanding 25
   Make a Time Line 27

Post-Lunar Landing Space Exploration

   Important Events: 1969–1997 28
   Space Stations 30
   Activity #5: Understanding Orbits 33
   Activity #6: Understanding Orbits II 34
   Activity #7: Understanding Orbits III 35
   Vomit Comet: Understanding Free-Fall.... 36
   Activity #8: Understanding Free-Fall 37
   Space Shuttle 38
   Activity #9: How Big Are Space Ships? ... 39

Unmanned Missions to the Planets

   Pioneer 41
   Voyager 42
   Galileo 43
   Magellan 44
   Cassini 45

Mars

   Mars—Two Views 46
   Mars................................ 47
   Martian Orbit 48
   Activity #10: Martian Orbit 49
   Activity #11: Artistic Martian Orbit 51
   Retrograde Motion 52
   Activity #12: Retrograde Motion 54

Unmanned Missions to Mars

   Chronology 57
   USSR/Russia Missions 58
   Mariner 59
   Viking 60
   Mars *Observer* 61
   Mars *Pathfinder* 62
   Pathfinder's Journey 66
   Activity #13: Hitting a Moving Target 67
   Activity #14: Time Delay 68
   Global Surveyor 71
   Activity #15: Capturing the Satellite...... 73
   Future Missions to Mars 74

Life on Mars?

   Early Views on Life 75
   Mars Meteorite 76

Astronomy and Space Science Report 77

Technology Connections 78

Resources 80

Introduction

Pick up any newspaper or magazine and you are bound to read something about America's return to Mars or the developments aboard the Russian Space Station, *Mir*. NASA reported more "hits" to its Mars *Pathfinder* Web site on July 5th, 1997, (the day after the *Pathfinder* landed on Mars) than were recorded on the Olympic Games Web site on opening day in Atlanta in 1996! Space is the place, and space is HOT!

As teachers, we are keenly aware that our students' attention is often directed toward recent events and that our lessons need to reflect real-world applications in order for students to appreciate their relevance. It is not always possible to do this, of course. The three R's, for example, are very important but are often arduous to teach and to learn. Fortunately, recent developments in space have provided science teachers with an exciting opportunity in their efforts to teach astronomy and space science.

This book is designed for teachers who want to cash in on some of the exciting developments in space as a way of getting across to students a very important curriculum—astronomy and space exploration. Both the fifth grade and eighth grade curricula require an astronomy component, and this book will help teachers with the background they need in order to effectively teach these concepts as well as several ideas they can implement immediately in the classroom. The book will focus on the manned and unmanned missions into space which have led us to our present-day attempts at learning more about Mars and our solar system.

The background information in this book is intended for the teacher, but the information and Web sites may be shared directly with the students as they work on their astronomy/space science projects (see page 77). Teachers will find information on a variety of subjects as well as a number of Web sites which will go into more depth.

This is indeed an exciting time to be teaching astronomy. All of our students were born after the manned moon landings, and many of our students were born after the Space Shuttle *Challenger* accident in 1986. It is so very important to make students aware of where we have been and where we should be going in the future of space exploration. Many of our students will have careers directly or indirectly tied to the space program. To that end, this book is dedicated to exploring several issues in astronomy and space science. Enjoy!

© Teacher Created Materials, Inc.   #2383 Exploring Mars and Beyond—Challenging

Early Space Exploration

Birth of Space Exploration

During World War II, Nazi Germany was striking terror into the heart of Great Britain with its V-2 rockets designed by rocket engineers in Peenemunde, Germany. These rockets were able to carry an explosive payload across the English Channel from bases in France and land in the middle of Britain. Rockets would change the face of war forever.

With the fall of Nazi Germany in 1945, both the United States and the Soviet Union were interested in getting their hands on the rocket designers of the V-2. Each country knew that the future victors of any war would need to have air superiority through rockets. As the United States forces closed in from the West and the Soviet forces closed in from the East, the rocket scientists were found and taken to one of the two countries.

What the United States and Soviet Union may or may not have counted on, however, was the fact that these same rocket scientists of the Nazi war machine were actually interested in a completely different application of their designs. The scientists were interested in building rockets capable of escaping Earth's gravity and traveling out into the solar system. They had been forced to build rockets for mass destruction while under the Nazi rule, but now they had high hopes for a space program.

In 1957, 12 years after the fall of Nazi Germany, the United States awoke one morning to find the Soviet Union had beaten them into outer space with a small satellite known as *Sputnik* (which means "fellow traveler" or "companion" in Russian). As *Sputnik* orbited the planet every 95 minutes, it launched a war which would last longer than World War II. This was the war in space! Who would be first in space? With a Cold War raging between the United States and USSR, it became of paramount importance to be first in space.

The story of the exploration of space is also the story of competition. Two countries with mutual distrust for one another were locked in a fierce battle to get ahead. But without this battle, who knows if a manned moon landing would ever have occurred. As you read the following pages (6–26), you will see how the United States and the Soviet Union raced against each other in the quest for space. Through a series of unmanned and then manned missions into outer space, the United States and the Soviet Union were waging a huge public relations battle with one another. Funding for the space programs was quite high in an effort to be first.

As the story continues into the 1990s, however, some major changes have occurred. The most important change has been the collapse of the Soviet Union. Now, without an opponent and certainly without an opponent with much money, the face of the space race has changed dramatically. We have gone from a period of competition to a period of cooperation. Will the United States and Russia (part of the former Soviet Union) be able to make great achievements in space as partners instead of competitors? Only the future holds the answer.

Early Space Exploration

Important Events: 1926–1969

Date	Events
1926	Robert Goddard launches first liquid-fueled rocket.
1945	Wernher von Braun defects from Nazi Germany to United States.
10/4/57	Soviet Union launches *Sputnik*, first man-made satellite in space.
11/3/57	*Sputnik 2* carries the first living passenger into space—a dog. (USSR)
2/1/58	United States enters the space race with *Explorer 1*. (first U.S. satellite)
1/4/59	*Luna 1* satellite is the first satellite to fly by the moon. (USSR)
9/15/59	*Luna 2* becomes first man-made object to crash-land on the moon. (USSR)
4/12/61	Yuri Gagarin becomes first man in space. (USSR)
4/17/61	U.S. attempts unsuccessfully to overthrow Soviet-supported Castro government in Cuba.
5/5/61	Alan Shepard, Jr., becomes first American man in space.
4/26/62	*Ranger 4* becomes first U.S. craft to crash land on the moon.
6/16/63	Valentina Tereshkova becomes first woman astronaut. (USSR)
3/18/65	Alexi Leonov becomes first man to walk in space. (USSR)
6/3/65	Ed White becomes first American to walk in space.
2/3/66	*Luna 9* becomes first spacecraft ever to make a soft landing on the moon and transmit data back to Earth. (USSR)
5/30/66	*Surveyor 1* becomes U.S.A.'s first successful soft lunar lander.
1/27/67	*Apollo 1* fire kills three American astronauts.
4/23/67	Test flight of the Soviet's *Soyuz* rocket kills cosmonaut on re-entry.
10/18/67	*Venera 4* spacecraft is first to enter the atmosphere of Venus. (USSR)
9/15/68	*Zond 5* becomes first spacecraft to perform a lunar flyby and return to Earth. (USSR)
11/10/68	*Zond 6* becomes first spacecraft containing living organisms to perform a lunar flyby and return to Earth. (USSR)
12/21/68	*Apollo 8* becomes first manned spacecraft to orbit moon and return to Earth. (USA)
7/20/69	*Apollo 11* lands first men on the moon. (USA)
7/21/69	*Luna 15* crash lands on the moon as *Apollo 11* astronauts walk on moon.

Early Space Exploration

Robert Goddard and Wernher von Braun

Rocket Designers

Robert Goddard (1882–1945)

Truly a space exploration visionary, Robert Goddard is credited in 1926 with designing and launching the first rocket engines to use liquid fuel. Before Goddard, rockets had been designed and launched with solid fuel only. His design mixed gasoline with liquid oxygen to provide thrust. He even wrote a book proposing the development of a rocket which could reach the moon, an unimaginable thought in his day. In fact, Goddard was criticized once in a newspaper editorial for believing that rockets would be able to function in outer space.

"Professor Goddard does not know the relation between action and reaction and the need to have something better than a vacuum against which to react. He seems to lack the basic knowledge ladled out daily in high schools."

—New York Times, 1921

Undaunted, Goddard continued with his research, and today we know he was correct in his theories.

Wernher von Braun (1912–1977)

While Goddard worked on his rocket designs for the United States, Germany had its own rocket scientist in Wernher von Braun. During World War II, von Braun helped Nazi Germany develop the destructive V-2 rockets. These rockets were also powered by gasoline and liquid oxygen but were intended for military purposes. Finally, in 1945, as Germany was in the final days of the Nazi regime, von Braun led a group of German scientists to surrender to the incoming American forces. He knew their skills would be needed by the Americans, and he had plans to persuade the United States to launch rockets into outer space.

In America, von Braun again began designing rockets for military purposes, but soon after the Soviet Union launched *Sputnik*, von Braun found himself working full time for a new organization called the National Aeronautics and Space Administration (NASA). From 1960 until his death in 1977, von Braun was the driving force behind rocket-assisted space exploration.

Early Space Exploration

Goddard and von Braun—Check for Understanding

Now that you are familiar with the history behind the development of modern rocketry and the story of two of modern rocketry's key designers, read and respond to the following questions:

1. What role did war play in the development of the space program?

   _____
   _____
   _____

2. The editorial in the *New York Times* criticized Goddard for not understanding basic high school physics in his ideas for space travel. Knowing what we know today about space travel, how would you respond to the author of that editorial?

   _____
   _____
   _____

3. Have you ever been told by someone that an idea of yours was impossible, yet you were able to make it happen anyway? Briefly describe your idea and how you overcame the odds.

   _____
   _____
   _____

4. Wernher von Braun initially used his talents as a rocket scientist to develop military weapons for Germany and the United States. Later in his life, von Braun created rockets for the peaceful exploration of space. How should history judge von Braun? Consider all of the circumstances he faced during his life. (You might want to do some more research on von Braun before responding).

   _____
   _____
   _____

Early Space Exploration

Activity #1: Air-Powered Rocket Launch

Robert Goddard and Wernher von Braun were pioneers in the field of modern rocketry. Both men designed rockets which used liquid fuel to power their flight. The following activity is designed to introduce your students to the fundamentals of rocketry by allowing them to create their own air-powered rocket. This activity is the first in a series of activities which will parallel the story of space exploration.

Materials

- long balloons
- string
- drinking straws
- masking tape

Procedure

1. Stretch a length of string across the classroom or out on the playground.
2. Before tying the second end of the string, thread a straw onto the string.
3. Have a student inflate a balloon and tape it to the straw as shown below.
4. Release the balloon.

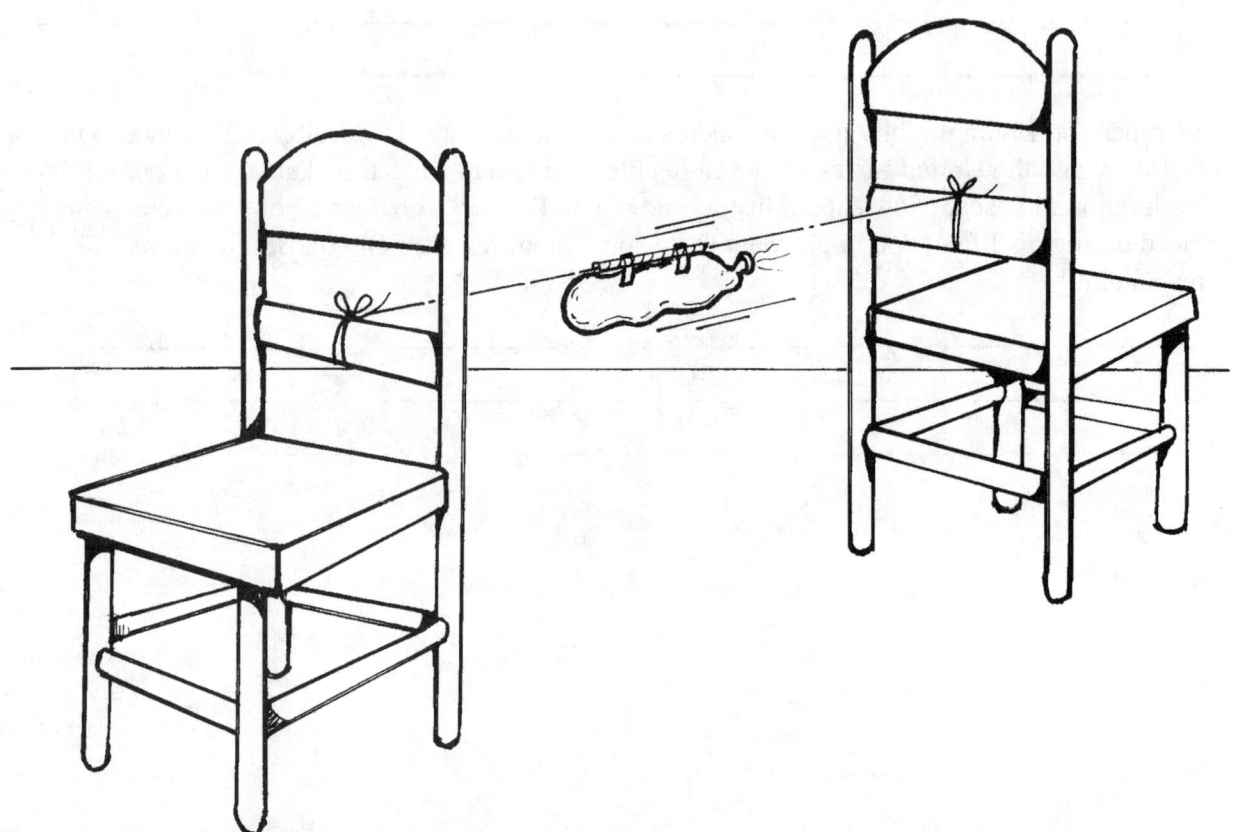

Early Space Exploration

Activity #1: Air-Powered Rocket Launch *(cont.)*

Discussion

Rockets work on the principle of Newton's third law. For every action, there is an equal and opposite reaction. The action of the air rushing out of a balloon causes an equal force in the opposite direction, and the balloon zips off along the string.

There are two basic fuels used in rockets: solid fuel and liquid fuel. The balloon rockets are gas powered, and while this demonstrates the principles of rocketry, it is important to understand that rockets used in space exploration use either solid or liquid fuel.

Drawings of a solid-fueled and a liquid-fueled rocket are provided below. Notice that a liquid-fueled rocket combines liquid hydrogen and oxygen in a combustion (explosive) reaction to form H_2O (water). When the space shuttle takes off, its liquid-fueled rockets are spewing out tons of steam! In outer space, there is no air and therefore no oxygen to combine with the hydrogen fuel. For this reason, rockets must carry their own oxygen in their engines to allow for combustion of fuel.

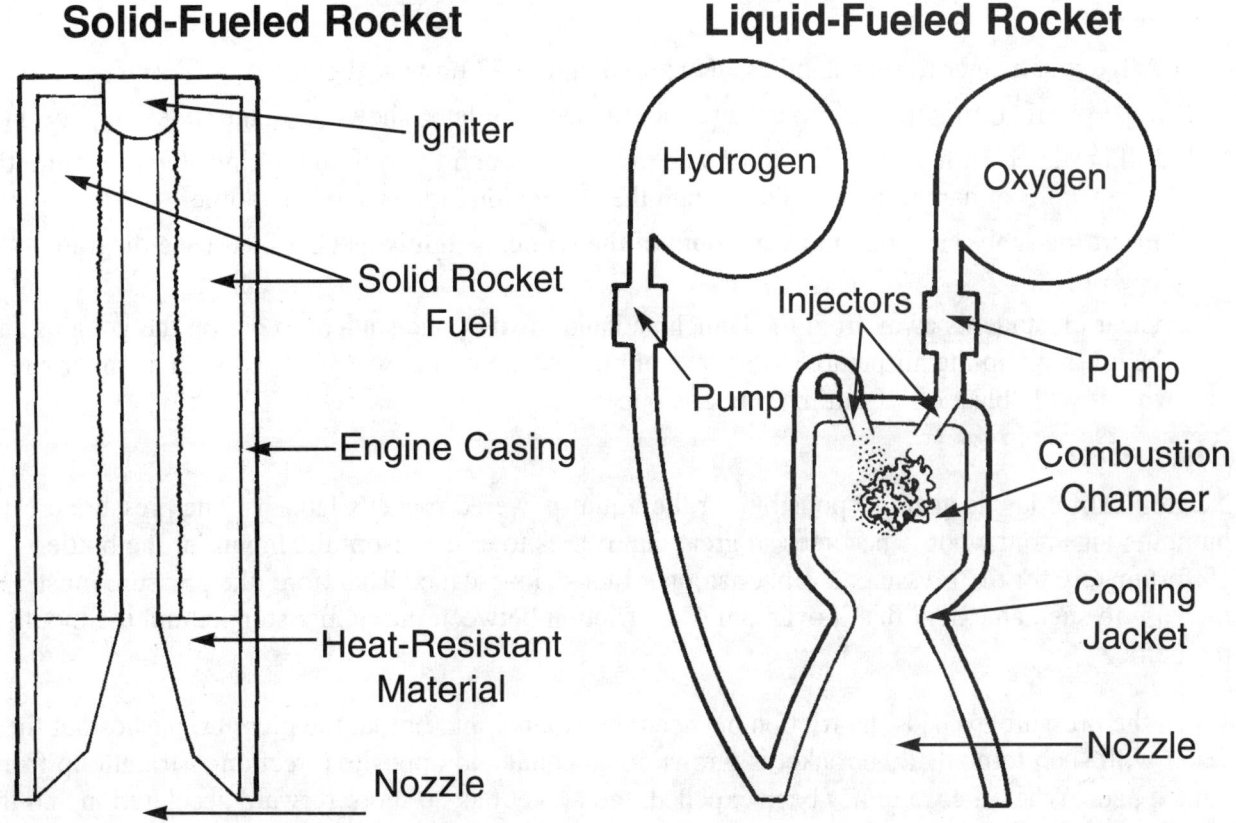

Extension

Have students inflate their balloons to various sizes and take notice of any differences in the distance they travel and the speed at which they travel. (*They should notice that smaller balloons travel faster but might not go as far as larger balloons. This is because the smaller balloon will experience less air resistance.*) Rocket design engineers must provide enough fuel for a rocket to arrive at its destination in space but not so much fuel that the rocket is too heavy to get off the launch pad.

© Teacher Created Materials, Inc.

Early Space Exploration

Activity #2: Liquid-Powered Rocket Launch

In the previous activity, your students had the opportunity to launch air-powered rockets. In the following activity, students will launch a water-powered rocket.

Materials

- rubber stopper (size: number 4)
- air pump
- stopwatch
- plastic drinking straw
- protective goggles for eyes
- air pump needle
- ring stand
- two-liter plastic soda bottle
- metal clothes hanger

Procedure

1. Push an air pump needle through the center of the rubber stopper as shown in diagram #1 on page 11.
2. Affix coat hanger to ring stand as shown in diagram #2 on page 11.
3. Tape plastic drinking straw to a 2-liter plastic soda bottle as shown in diagram #3 on page 11.
4. Fill bottle about half full with water and invert it through the ring in the ring stand. Ensure that the metal coat hanger is inserted through the straw along the side of the bottle.
5. Insert the rubber stopper into the mouth of the bottle as tightly as possible. (See diagram #4 on page 11.)
6. Clear all students away from the launch pad and instruct one student to put on the goggles and begin to pump the air pump. After several pumps, the rocket will be filled with so much pressure that it will "blast off" from the rubber stopper.

Discussion

Newton's third law is again responsible for the liquid-powered rocket's launch. The pressure created by pumping air into the bottle becomes so great that it tries to escape from the mouth of the bottle. Unfortunately for the pressure, a rubber stopper blocks its escape. Therefore, the pressure must increase to such an extent that it overcomes the friction between the rubber stopper and the mouth of the bottle.

When the pressure exceeds the friction between the stopper and bottle, the pressure pushes out the water with such force that the rocket is thrown in an equal and opposite direction—straight up from the launch pad. When the water has been expelled, the rocket has no more forward acceleration and then falls back to Earth.

Encourage your students to try varying amounts of water in the rocket. They will find that too much water makes the rocket too heavy on takeoff, and too little will not provide enough thrust to achieve a great height. Experiment until you find the proper amount to achieve the greatest height. You can measure height by timing the flight with a stopwatch.

Early Space Exploration

Activity #2: Liquid-Powered Rocket Launch *(cont.)*

Diagrams #1–4 of Water-Powered Rocket Launch

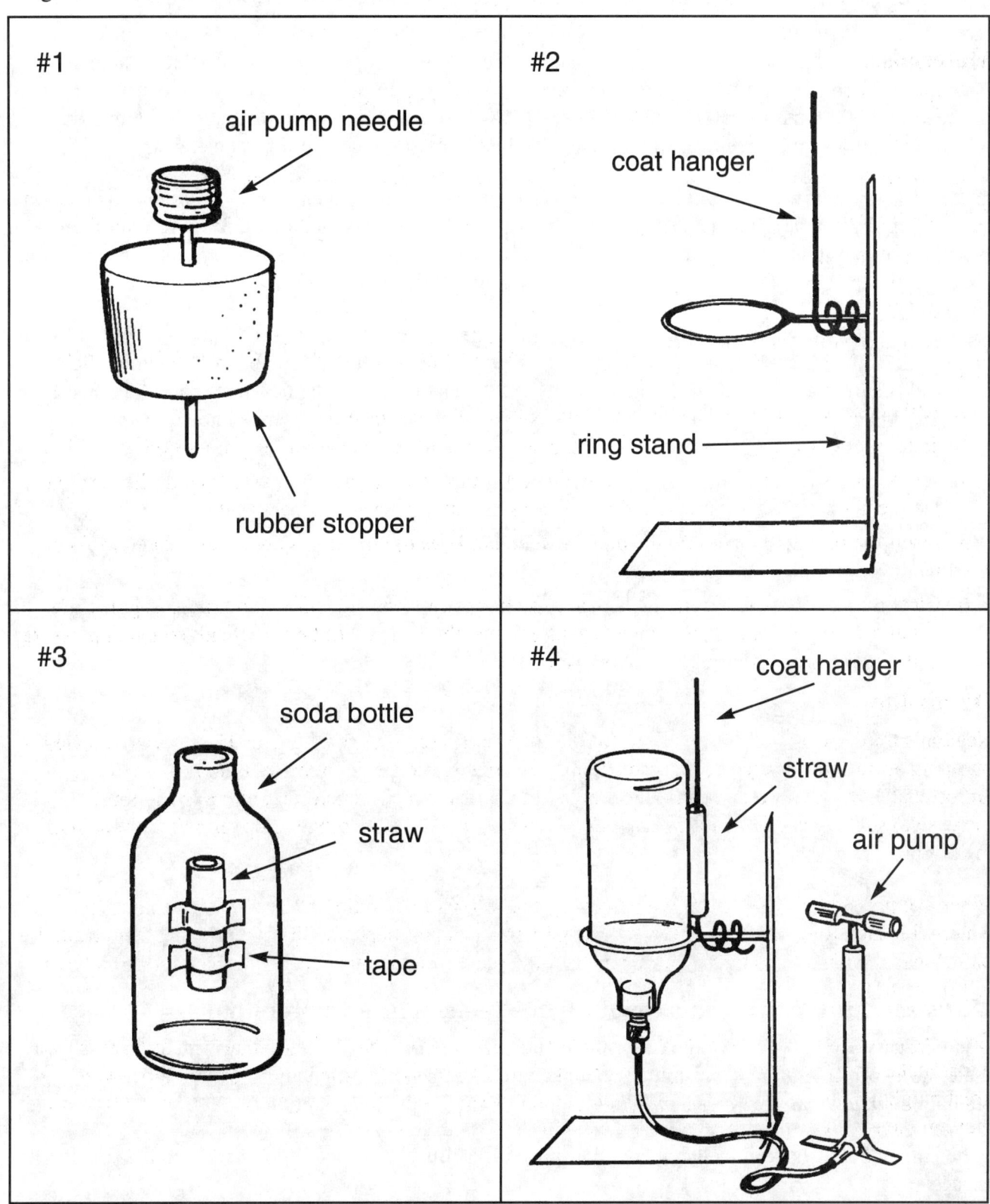

Early Space Exploration

Sputnik and Explorer

The Beginning of the Space Race

Sputnik http://www.nauts.com/histpace/vehicles/histsputnik.html

Launched on October 4, 1957, *Sputnik 1* officially launched the space race. The German rocket scientists who had gone over to the Soviet Union after the war were the first to succeed in launching a satellite into orbit around Earth. Every 95 minutes, *Sputnik 1* completed one revolution around Earth at a speed of 29,000 km/h (18,000 mph). *Sputnik 1* was 58 cm (22 inches) in diameter and emitted an electronic radio signal "beep" for three weeks. It finally crashed back to Earth on January 4, 1958.

Sputnik 1 was followed by *Sputnik 2*, which was launched on November 3, 1957. *Sputnik 2* carried the first living organism, Laika the dog, into space. Sadly, the Russians had no ability to recover their satellites at that time, and Laika died in orbit when her air supply ran out. *Sputnik 2* itself remained in space until April 14, 1958, when Earth's gravity finally pulled it out of orbit.

Sputnik 1 and *2* awoke the American space program. If the Soviet Union could launch a dog into space, surely they could launch a nuclear warhead into space. This was not acceptable to the United States' national security, and President Eisenhower created the National Aeronautics and Space Administration (NASA) in an effort to compete with the Soviets. America needed its presence known in space!

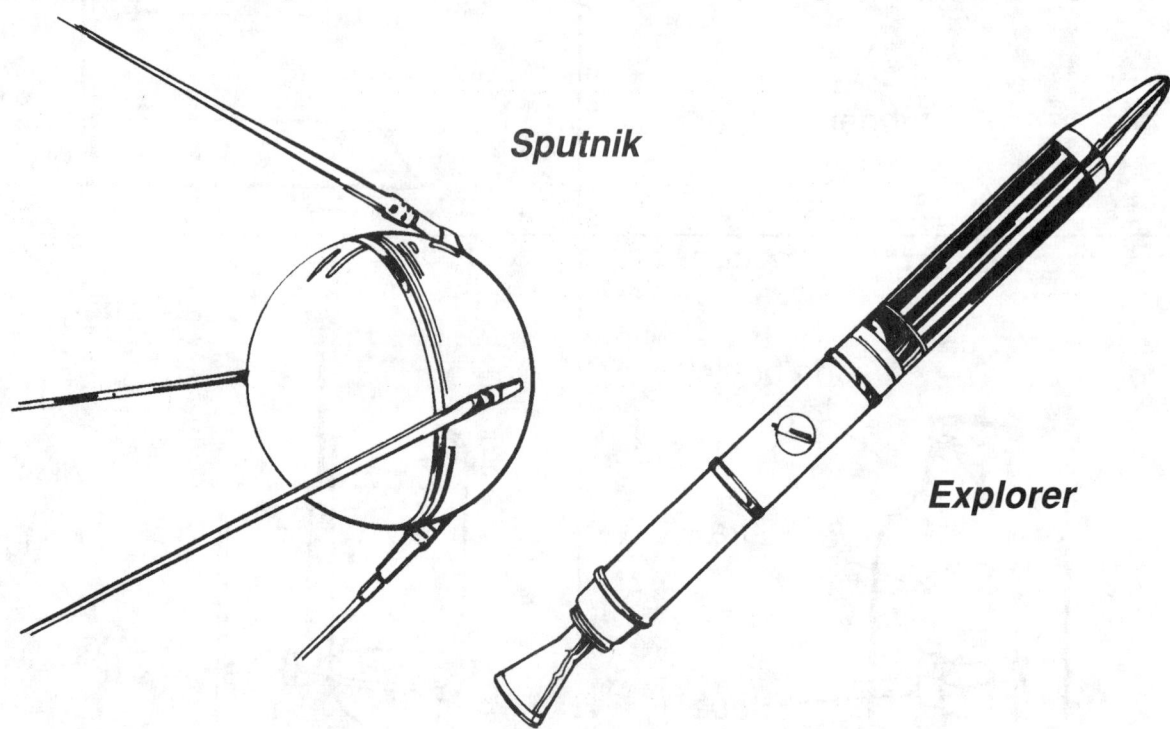

Explorer http://www.nauts.com/histpace/vehicles/histexplorer.html

On February 1, 1958, four months after the launch of *Sputnik 1*, the United States finally had its own satellite in orbit. *Explorer* transmitted data back to scientists on Earth and discovered a belt of radiation—known as the *Van Allen Belt*—trapped by the Earth's magnetic field.

The United States had officially entered the space race. But the Soviet Union had been the first in space.

Early Space Exploration

Activity #3: Newton's Third Law

Space travel is dependent upon Newton's Third Law of Motion. Newton noticed that for every physical action, there was an equal physical reaction in the opposite direction. This activity will further your students' understanding of Newton's Third Law.

Materials
- two rulers
- six pennies

Procedure
1. Tape the rulers flat on the surface of the table and line up the pennies between the rulers as shown in the diagram. The pennies should be touching one another.
2. Using your index finger, move one penny back away from the row of pennies by about six inches.
3. Using your index finger, quickly slide the single penny back into the row of pennies.

Drawing of Activity

Discussion

When the penny slides into the row of pennies, that is the action. The reaction in the opposite direction is the penny on the opposite end moving away from the row of pennies. Try moving two pennies away from the row and then quickly sliding them back into the row of pennies. Do you notice that now two pennies on the opposite side will move away from the row of pennies?

Newton's Third Law states that for every action there is an equal and opposite reaction. Rockets need to spew out as much weight of fuel as the weight of the rocket in order to get the rocket off the ground. But the thrust of the rocket engines must exceed the weight of the rocket itself in order to get it up to orbital speed. In order to achieve orbit around Earth like the *Sputnik* satellite, a rocket must provide enough thrust to make the satellite travel at over 27,000 km/hr (17,000 mph).

Early Space Exploration

Luna and *Ranger*

First Unmanned Probes to Land on the Moon

Luna http://www.nauts.com/histpace/vehicles/histluna.html

Both the United States and the Soviet Union had successfully entered the space race by putting satellites (*Sputnik* and *Explorer*) in orbit around Earth. With the *Luna* project, the Soviet Union had its sights on the next great challenge—sending a probe to land on the moon! On January 2, 1959, the Soviet Union launched *Luna 1* on its way to the moon. *Luna 1* reached the moon on January 4 and, among other things, discovered the moon lacked a magnetic field (although Earth has one) and that the sun emitted a "solar wind" into the solar system. *Luna 1* did not, however, land on the moon itself.

Project *Luna* was finally successful in its mission to impact on the moon in September 1959 with *Luna 2*. *Luna 2* became the first object to land on the moon (albeit a crash landing). It would be almost seven years before a spacecraft was able successfully to land on the moon. *Luna 9* holds the honor of being the very first spacecraft ever to land softly on the surface of the moon (it landed on February 3, 1966) and transmit photographic data back to Earth. It was obvious to the United States that the Soviet Union was sending the *Luna* probes to the moon in preparation for a future manned lunar landing. And it was obvious that there was a lot of catching up to do.

Ranger http://www.nauts.com/histpace/vehicles/histranger.html

Never far behind, the United States launched its own program to land a probe on the surface of the moon. The probe was known as *Ranger*. *Ranger 1* was launched on August 23, 1961, but its mission was only to check out the operation systems of the orbiter, and it never left Earth's orbit. It wasn't until the launch of *Ranger 3* on January 26, 1962, that the United States sent a probe to land on the moon. It had now been a little less than three years since the Soviet Union's *Luna 2* had crash-landed on the moon. The United States was far behind. Unfortunately, *Ranger 3* missed the moon by 37,000 km (23,000 mi) and is now orbiting the sun. The Soviet Union was securely in the lead!

But *Ranger 4* successfully impacted on the lunar surface on April 26, 1962. The United States had finally arrived on the moon! The *Ranger* program continued to launch probes to the moon until 1965 when it was replaced by the *Surveyor* Lunar Lander program.

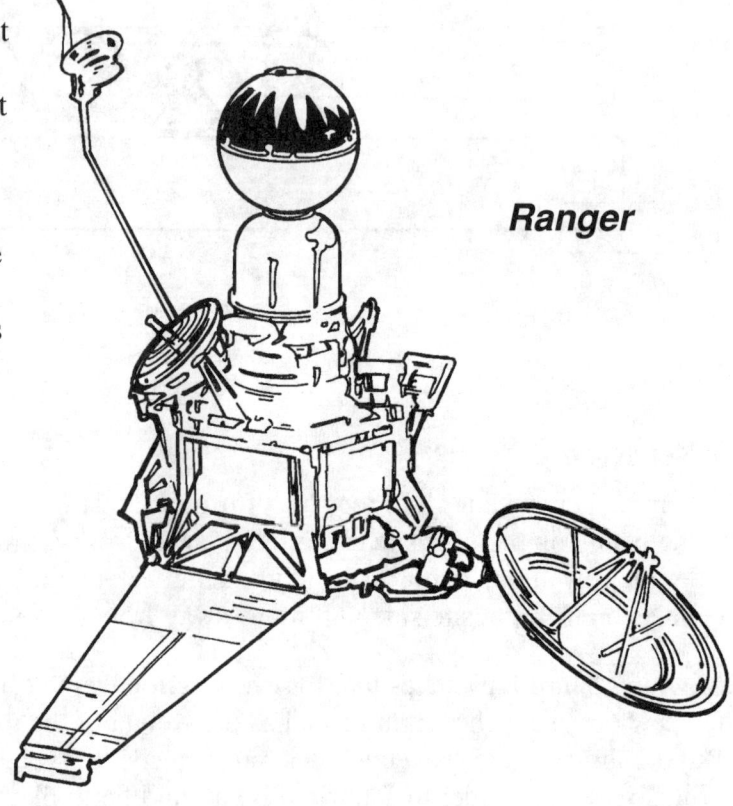

Ranger

Early Space Exploration

Searching for Astronauts

After the dramatic launch of the Soviet *Sputnik* in 1957, it became clear to the United States that not only were the Soviets interested in launching satellites into space, they were also interested in launching people into space. Thus, in 1958 the newly created National Aeronautics and Space Administration (NASA) began actively recruiting military test pilots to become the first astronauts.

At this time, no one knew if people could even survive in space. Laika, the dog, had lived for a short time aboard *Sputnik 2*, but she had not been expected to re-enter Earth's atmosphere. Could people be launched into space and be safely returned to Earth? In 1958 the question went unanswered, yet hundreds of people answered NASA's call for volunteers.

On April 9, 1959, NASA introduced the first seven astronauts to the public. These seven men would be a part of America's first journey into space during the *Mercury* program. The seven astronauts were Alan Shepard, Jr., Deke Slayton, John Glenn, Wally Schirra, Scott Carpenter, Gordon Cooper, and Gus Grissom.

Some of the qualifications to become one of the original seven astronauts are listed below. Ask your students about these qualifications. Are most of them fair? What qualifications do you agree with, and which would you change? Are there any other qualifications you think should have been added? Why do you think NASA imposed a height and weight requirement? (The *Mercury* capsule was very tiny!)

Original Qualifications

- Candidates must be men.
- Candidates must have a minimum of 1,500 flight hours.
- Candidates must have jet pilot training.
- Candidates must possess at least a bachelor's degree.
- Candidates must pass national security requirements.
- Candidates must not be taller than five feet eleven inches.
- Candidates must weigh less than 180 pounds.
- Candidates must be under 40 years of age.

Today, the qualifications for becoming an astronaut are quite different. Both men and women are recruited to become astronauts, and there is no longer a height requirement. You can find out more about becoming an astronaut at the following Web pages:

Ask an Astronaut **http://www.nss.org/askastro**

The Astronaut Connection **http://www.nauts.com**

Early Space Exploration

Vostok and Mercury

First Manned Missions in Space

Vostok http://www.nauts.com/histpace/vehicles/histvostok.html

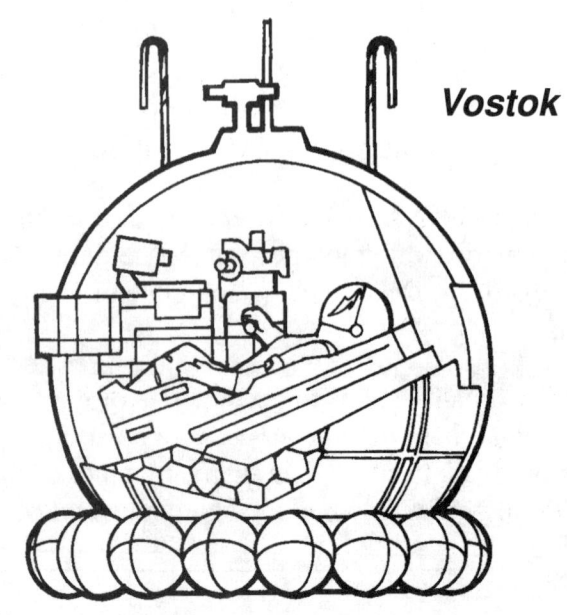
Vostok

It wasn't long after the launch of unmanned space probes that the Soviet Union and United States turned their attention to manned space flight. The Soviets had launched Laika the dog with *Sputnik 2* in 1957, and on April 12, 1961, they launched Yuri Gagarin atop an ICBM (inter-continental ballistic missile) refitted for human flight and retitled *Vostok 1*. Gagarin's flight lasted almost two hours, and he orbited Earth one time. The *Vostok* program would last until the flight of the first woman in space—Valentina Tereshkova on June 16, 1963. She also was the last person to ever fly into space alone!

Mercury http://www.nauts.com/histpace/vehicles/histmercury.html

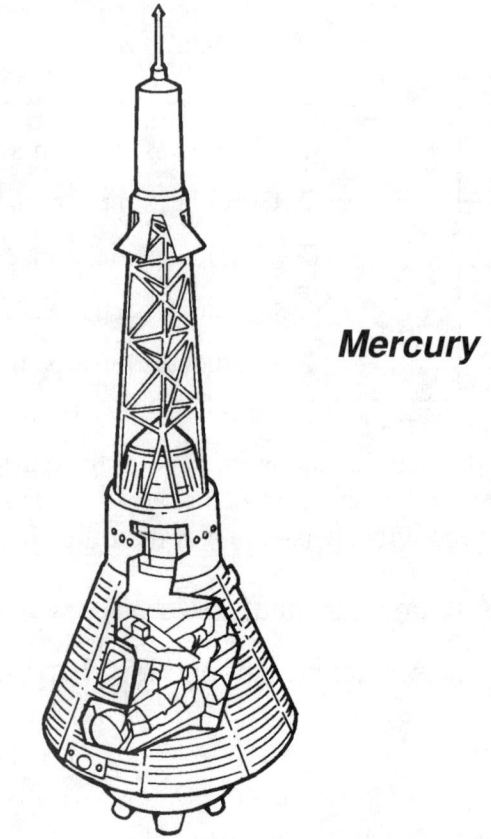
Mercury

Prompted by the success of Gagarin's flight as well as the botched Bay of Pigs invasion of Cuba on April 17, 1961, President Kennedy put his full support behind the space program in an effort to reaffirm America's presence as a world leader. On May 5, 1961, Alan Shepard, Jr., took America's manned space program into space for the very first time. His 15-minute flight launched project *Mercury*, a series of six solo manned missions into space. Project *Mercury* ended with Gordon Cooper's flight on May 15, 1963. Cooper flew 22 revolutions around Earth in a day and a half and would be the last American to fly into space alone.

Early Space Exploration

Activity #4: Egg Drop

Coming in for a Landing

The single most important aspect of manned space flight must be the safety of the crew members. Because they were launched atop intercontinental ballistic missiles originally intended to propel nuclear warheads at an enemy, a number of modifications had to be made to rockets before they could carry men into space.

Some of the design modifications included a space capsule which would contain the astronauts atop the missile and a plan to get the capsule back to Earth safely. Today, the space shuttle launches into space like a rocket and glides back to Earth like an airplane. But in the early days of manned space flight, United States astronauts returned to Earth in a capsule suspended beneath parachutes which would then splash down in the ocean. And, even to this day, Russian cosmonauts return to Earth in parachuted capsules which come to a soft landing on the ground!

When the *Mercury* astronauts returned to Earth from space, they were plucked from the ocean along with their space capsule. The astronaut and his capsule were then returned to NASA by the United States Navy. But on the second *Mercury* mission, piloted by Gus Grissom on July 21, 1961, the emergency escape hatch blew open as Grissom awaited pickup in the ocean. Grissom had to scramble out of the spacecraft and into the water before he and the ship went under. To this day, that *Mercury* capsule is the only capsule of the *Mercury*, *Gemini*, and *Apollo* space programs lying on the bottom of the ocean.

In order for your students to appreciate the engineering necessary to bring astronauts home safely, the following activity on page 18 has been provided.

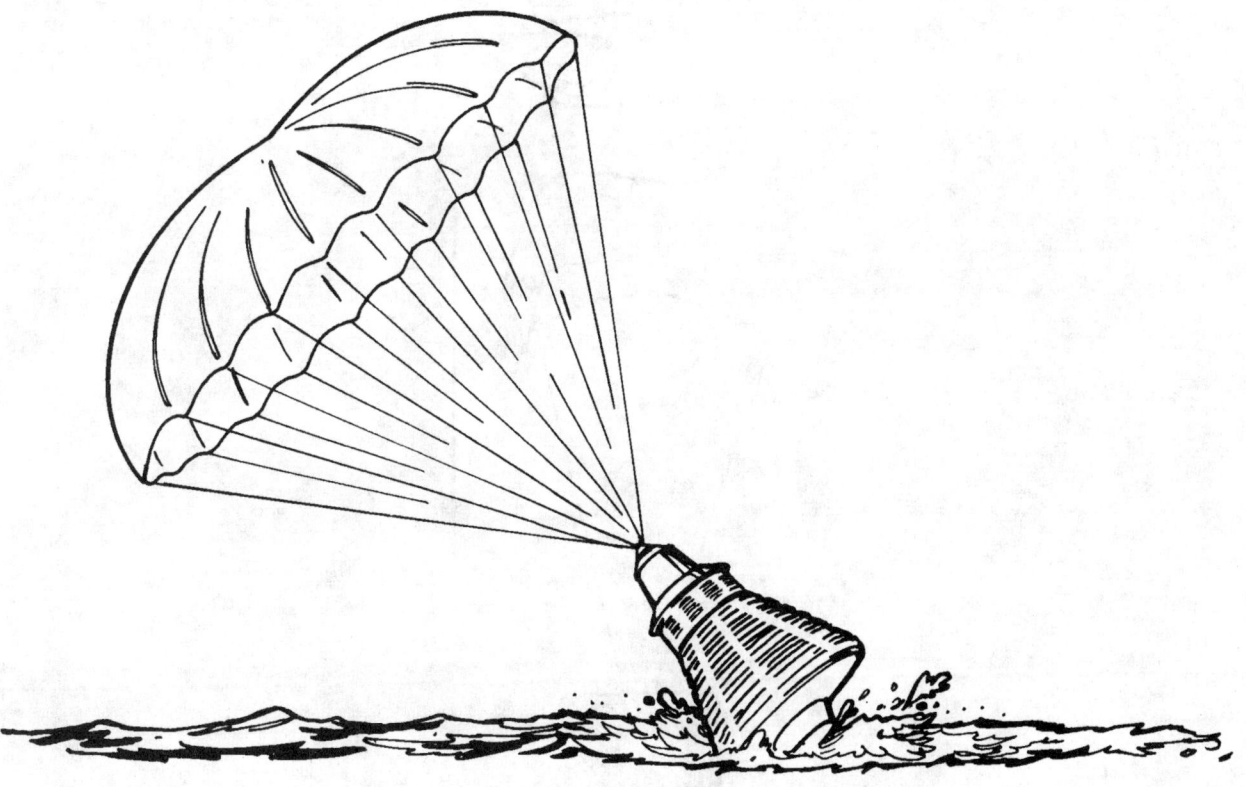

Early Space Exploration

Activity #4: Egg Drop *(cont.)*

Materials

- eggs
- bubble wrap
- newspaper
- Styrofoam peanuts
- Jello
- string
- whatever other "construction" materials you can acquire

Procedure

1. Tell students the story of how the early astronauts returned to Earth from space.
2. Ask students to design a landing craft which will allow for the safe landing of their "eggsperiment."
3. Take them to the pre-determined "drop site" before they begin so they know what they are up against.
4. Give prizes for most successful, most creative, most colorful, most destroyed, etc.

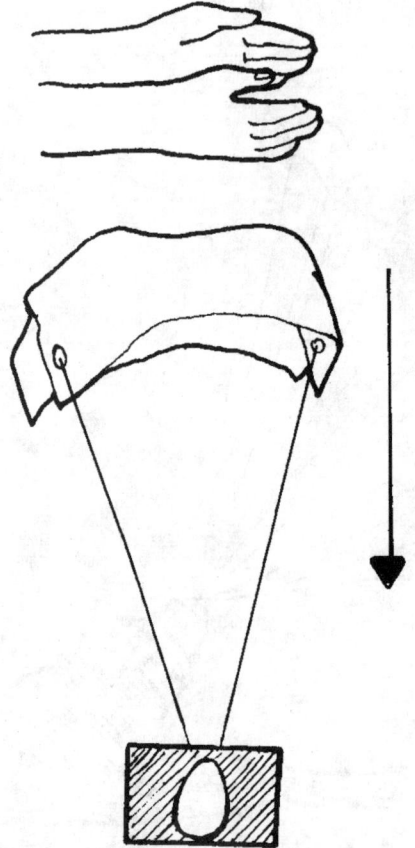

Early Space Exploration

Voskhod **and** *Gemini*

First Manned Missions into Space

Voskhod http://www.nauts.com/histpace/vehicles/histvoskhod.html

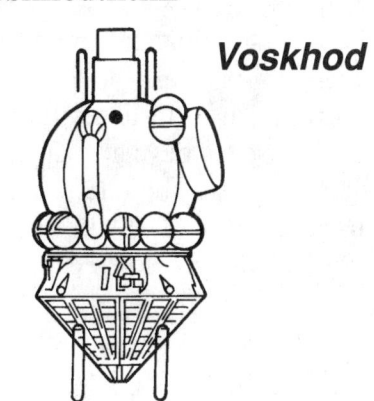

Voskhod

By October 1964, the Soviet Union had retired its *Vostok* one-man (and woman) crewed missions and had launched a rocket capable of carrying a two-man crew. This new rocket, named *Voskhod*, would be another first for the Soviets. Cosmonaut (a Soviet astronaut) Alexi Leonov became the first person to float freely in space on the second *Voskhod* mission on March 18, 1965.

Gemini http://www.nauts.com/histpace/ vehicles/histgemini.html

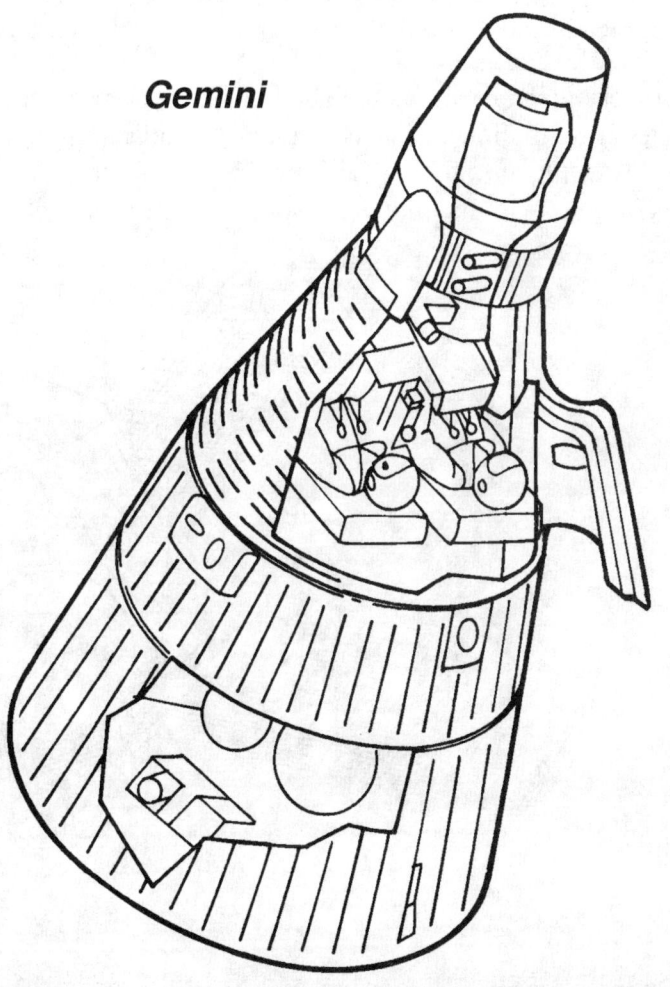

Gemini

Project *Gemini* got off the ground on March 23, 1965, with Gus Grissom and John Young as its astronauts. Project *Gemini* was the United States' attempt at putting a two-man crew in space. It was important to launch more than one person at a time into space if the United States was going to go to the moon. Project *Gemini* proved that astronauts could walk and dock in space. On June 3, 1965, Ed White stepped outside the *Gemini 4* space capsule and became the second man to walk in space. Subsequent missions of *Gemini* would be used to practice docking in space—a necessity for future lunar landings. Project *Gemini* ended on November 11, 1966, with the flight of Jim Lovell and Buzz Aldrin—two men who would go on to much fame in the *Apollo* moon landing program. Aldrin would become the second man to walk on the surface of the moon, and Lovell would become the first to fly around the moon in *Apollo 8*, as well as captain the crippled *Apollo 13* home safely.

The United States and Soviet Union were now locked in a fierce battle to be first in space. Already, the Soviets had put the first man and woman in space, accomplished the first space walk, and launched the first two-man crew.

Early Space Exploration

Venera **and** *Mariner*

First Unmanned Mission to Planets

Venera

While the Soviet Union and United States put manned missions into space, they also continued with their unmanned space explorations. Project *Venera* was designed to probe the mysteries of the planet Venus. *Venera 1* was unsuccessful in its mission. Ground controllers lost contact with it on February 19, 1961, only seven days after its launch. But on October 18, 1967, *Venera 4* successfully entered the Venusian atmosphere and released several instruments for atmospheric studies before it was crushed by the intense pressures. This was another first for the Soviets—first probe to enter the atmosphere of Venus. Project *Venera* would continue to launch a number of missions to Venus until 1983.

Mariner   http://www.jpl.nasa.gov/missions/mariner10

Venera was the Soviet's first interplanetary probe, and *Mariner* was the United States' first. Launched on July 22, 1962, *Mariner 1* was sent to fly by the planet Venus. But about five minutes into its flight, *Mariner 1* was destroyed by ground controllers as it veered off course. On December 14, 1962, *Mariner 2* would become the first spacecraft ever to successfully fly by the planet Venus. Finally, the Americans had a "first" in space—the first to successfully fly by and collect data from another planet.

Project *Mariner* would continue launching probes until *Mariner 10* in 1973. These probes went to investigate the inner planets: Mercury, Venus, and Mars. Some were successful, some were not, but project *Mariner* allowed the United States its first pictures of these three planets and prompted NASA to continue with its unmanned space program as well as its manned.

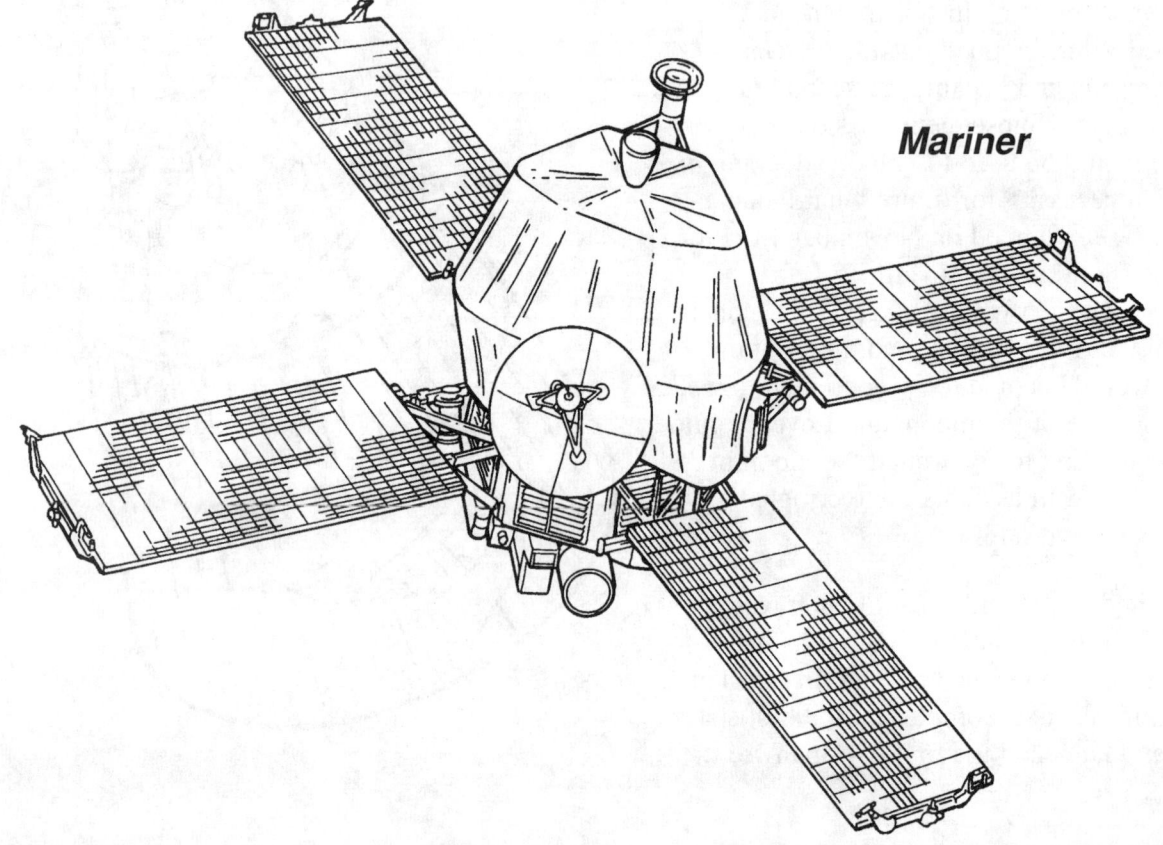
Mariner

Early Space Exploration

Surveyor and *Zond*

Unmanned Moon Probes

Zond

If people were going to walk on the moon, reliable mapping data would be needed in order to find suitable landing sites. Project *Zond* marked the Soviet Union's attempt at such an effort. *Zond 3* was launched on July 18, 1965, and on July 20 (exactly four years to the day before the first man would walk on the moon), *Zond 3* took 25 pictures (the first ever) of the far side of the moon. (Here on Earth, we always see the same side of the moon. Until *Zond 3*, no one had any idea how the far side would appear.)

The *Zond* missions continued, and in September 1968, *Zond 5* completed the very first lunar flyby and return to Earth. *Zond 5* zipped around the moon and headed back to Earth. The capsule contained a payload of living turtles, flies, mealworms, plants, and wine and landed safely on Earth on September 21, 1968. All on board were alive. It was very obvious now that the Soviet Union had the ability to fly people to the moon and back.

Surveyor   http://www.jpl.nasa.gov/missions/surveyor

Project *Surveyor* was the United States' effort to map the surface of the moon and perfect lunar landing in preparation for a manned landing. On May 30, 1966, *Surveyor 1* was launched and became the United States' first successful lunar lander. The Soviets had already successfully soft-landed *Luna 9* by this time (January 1966), so *Surveyor* did not accomplish a first.

The *Surveyor* program ended with *Surveyor 7* landing on January 10, 1968. With *Surveyor 7*, NASA was convinced it had enough information on landing and photographs of the lunar surface to attempt a manned landing.

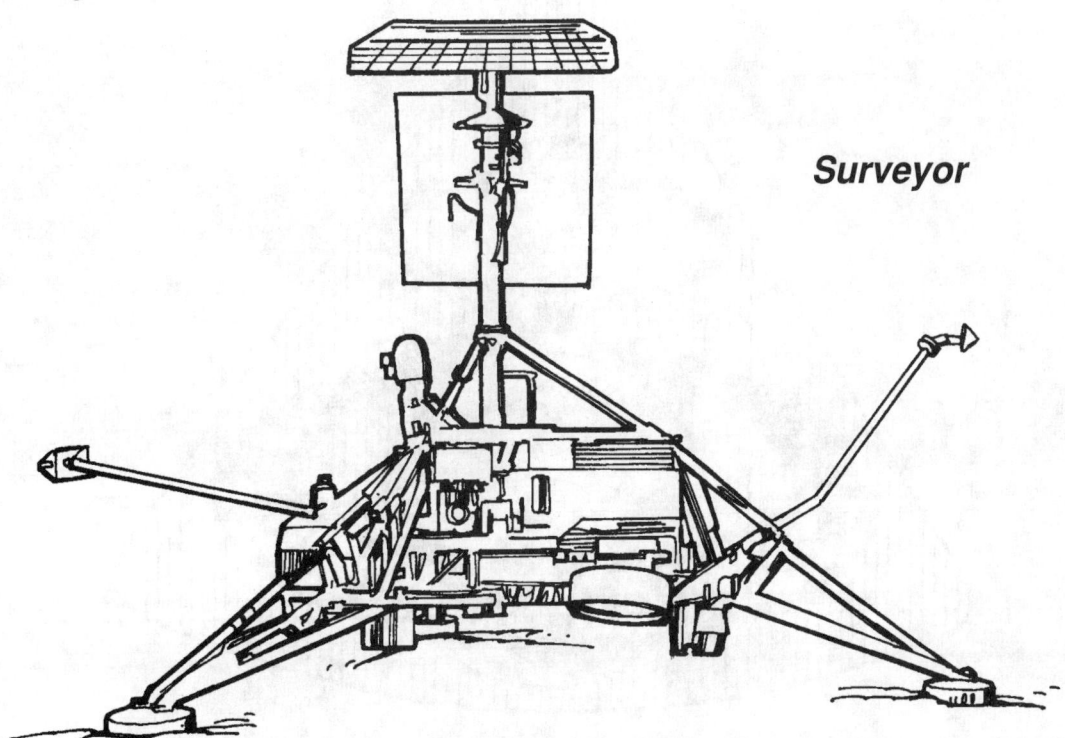

Surveyor

© *Teacher Created Materials, Inc.*   21   #2383 *Exploring Mars and Beyond—Challenging*

Early Space Exploration

Apollo and *Soyuz*

USA and USSR Battle for First Human Moon Landing

Apollo http://nssdc.gsfc.gov/planetary/lunar/apollo.html and

http://www.ksc.nasa.gov/history/apollo/apollo.html

President Kennedy had declared after Alan Shepard, Jr.'s mission in 1961 that America should go to the moon and be the first to do so. His stirring speech to the nation was seen as even more of a challenge to the people following his assassination in 1963. But by 1967, the United States was clearly in second place in the space race. Project *Apollo* was determined to push America back into the lead. *Apollo* was designed to take a three-man crew to the moon and return them to Earth.

But on January 27, 1967, tragedy struck the *Apollo* program. During a practice launch, a fire broke out in the cockpit of *Apollo 1*, killing its three astronauts: Gus Grissom (the second American in space and the first astronaut to fly in Project *Gemini*), Ed White (the first American to walk in space) and Roger Chaffee (a rookie astronaut). The fire hurt America's space program deeply but not its desire to continue in meeting President Kennedy's challenge to be first.

By December 1968, NASA felt that it had fixed the design problems in *Apollo* which had caused the accident in *Apollo 1* and was ready to shoot the moon! With the *Zond 3* spacecraft returning to Earth safely in September 1968, America knew that it was only a matter of time before the Soviets were sending people around the moon. It was time for action. On December 21, 1968, NASA embarked on a bold mission to send three astronauts (Frank Borman, Jim Lovell, and Bill Anders) around the moon on *Apollo 8*. These men would be the first ever to leave Earth's orbit and circumnavigate the moon. They would also become the turning point in the space race. America had its most important first!

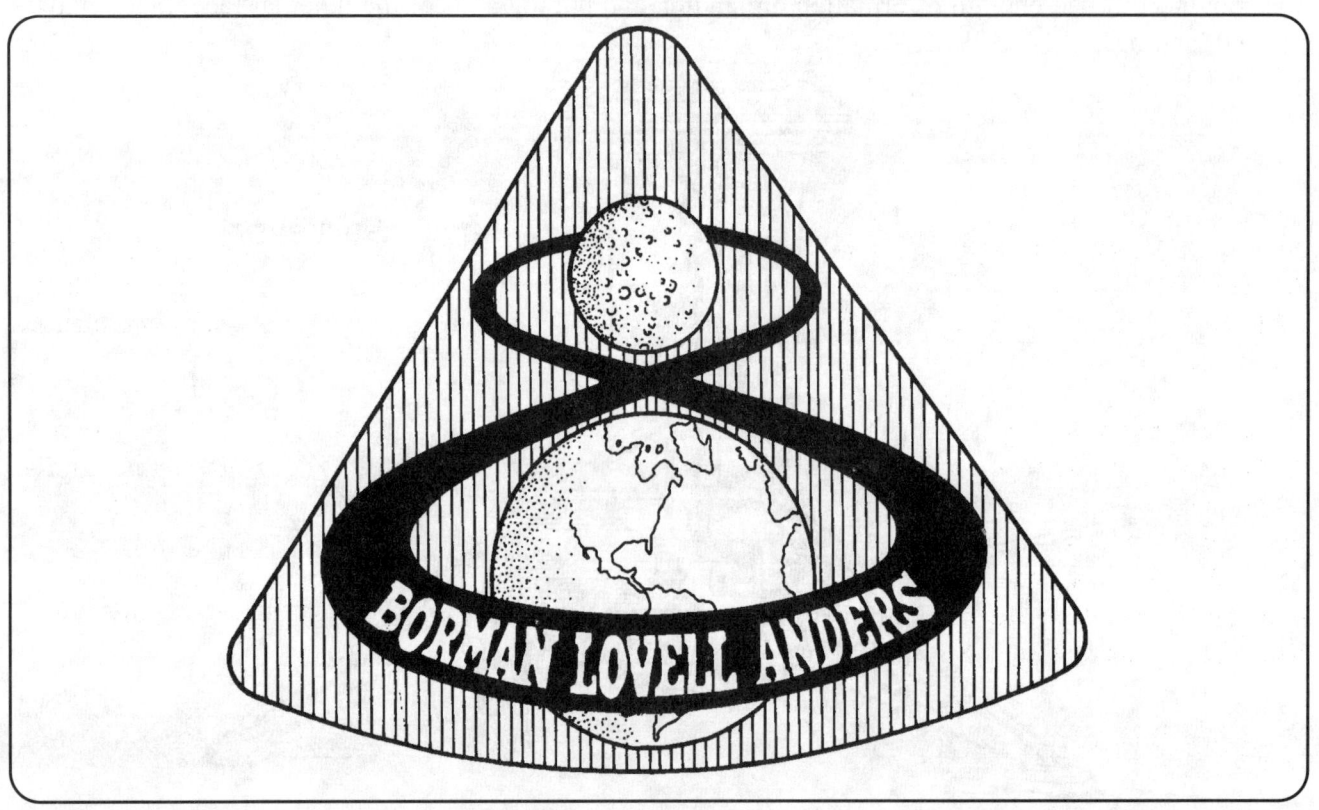

Early Space Exploration

Apollo and *Soyuz* (cont.)

USA and USSR Battle for First Human Moon Landing

Following the success of *Apollo 8*, NASA performed two more test missions to the moon before finally sending Neil Armstrong, Buzz Aldrin, and Michael Collins on *Apollo 11* in July of 1969. On July 20, 1969, Neil Armstrong and Buzz Aldrin became the first people ever to walk on the surface of the moon. The biggest prize in space had been won by the Americans.

First Humans to Walk on the Moon—July 20, 1969
Apollo 11: Neil Armstrong, Buzz Aldrin, Michael Collins
http://nssdc.gsfc.nasa.gov/planetary/lunar/apollo.html

All in all, 12 men would ultimately walk on the moon before December 1972. *Apollos 11, 12, 14, 15, 16,* and *17* were all successful landings (*Apollo 13* had to abort its planned lunar landing and return to Earth early). Gene Cernan of *Apollo 17* is the last person to have walked on the moon on December 14, 1972.

The following events further illustrate the fierce competition that took place in the race for the moon. As Neil and Buzz walked on the lunar surface, a Soviet unmanned probe, *Luna 15*, attempted to land on the moon and then take off to Earth with some lunar samples. This would provide the Soviets with the first lunar rock samples, even before *Apollo 11* could return to Earth with theirs. Unfortunately, *Luna 15* crashed onto the surface of the moon and was unable to complete its mission. Not until the unmanned *Luna 16* landed on the moon on September 20, 1970, were the Soviets successful in obtaining a lunar sample and returning it safely to Earth.

Early Space Exploration

Apollo and Soyuz (cont.)

USA and USSR Battle for First Human Moon Landing

Soyuz http://www.nauts.com/histpace/vehicles/histsoyuz.html

While the Americans had *Apollo*, the Soviets had *Soyuz*. The *Soyuz* rockets were designed to carry a crew of three to the moon.

Sadly, during the first test mission of a *Soyuz* around planet Earth, the test pilot, Vladamir Komarov, was killed when his spacecraft lost control in outer space and had to make an emergency landing back on Earth. The date was April 23, 1967, just three months after the tragic *Apollo 1* fire. Both the Soviet and American space programs were greatly affected by these tragedies. Finally, on October 26, 1968, the *Soyuz 2* spacecraft would be launched successfully into space and orbit around Earth. But with the December 1968 launch of a lunar bound *Apollo 8* and the July 1969 launch of lunar landing *Apollo 11*, the race to the moon would be over. Clearly, the challenge of landing a man successfully on the moon and returning him to Earth was a competition between two superpowers. One must wonder how or if humans would ever have made it to the moon without the events which transpired.

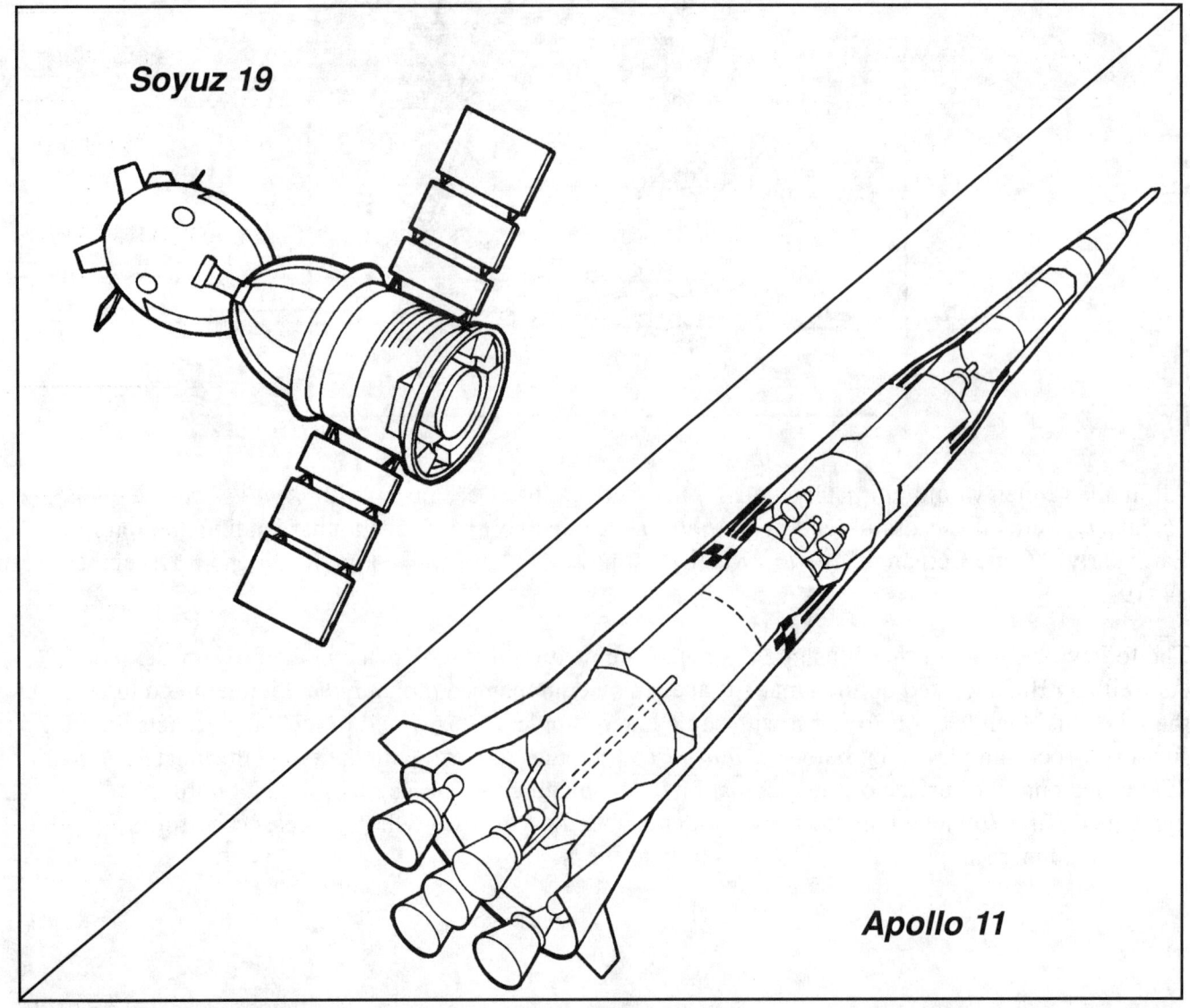

Early Space Exploration

Space Race—Check for Understanding

1. What event launched the space race between the Soviet Union and the United States? On what date did this event occur?

2. What was the first living organism in space, and what was its name?

3. What was the name of the first satellite launched by the United States? On what date did this launch occur?

4. What was the name of the first spacecraft to fly by the moon? Who launched it, and what was the date of its flyby?

5. What was the name of the first spacecraft to crash-land on the moon? Who launched it, and what was the date of its crash landing?

6. What was the name of the first American spacecraft to crash-land on the moon? When did this occur?

7. What was the name of the first man in space? What country launched him into orbit? What was the date of the launch?

8. What military crisis prompted President Kennedy to step up America's involvement in the space race?

9. What was the name of the first American in space? What was the date of his launch?

10. What was the name of the first woman in space? What was the date for her launch?

11. What was the name of the Soviet spacecraft designed to carry two people into space?

12. Who was the first man to float freely in space? What was the date of this event?

13. What was the name of the American spacecraft designed to carry two people into space?

Early Space Exploration

Space Race—Check for Understanding *(cont.)*

14. Who was the first American to float freely in space? What was the date of this event?

15. What was the name of the Soviet unmanned spacecraft sent to Venus? What was the name of the American unmanned spacecraft sent to Venus?

16. What was the name of the spacecraft designed by the Soviets to carry men to the moon?

17. What was the name of the spacecraft designed by the Americans to carry men to the moon?

18. What tragedy struck the American Lunar Landing project on January 27, 1967?

19. What tragedy struck the Soviet Lunar Landing project on April 23, 1967?

20. What was the name of the Soviet unmanned spacecraft sent to the moon in preparation for a manned moon landing? _____

21. Name at least one of the living creatures aboard a Soviet unmanned spacecraft sent around the moon and back to Earth in September 1968. _____

22. What was the name of the American unmanned spacecraft sent to land on the moon in preparation for a manned moon landing? _____

23. What was the name of the first manned mission to fly by the moon and return safely to Earth? What was the date of this event? _____

24. What was the name of the first manned mission to land on the moon and return safely to Earth? What was the date of this event? _____

25. What was *Luna 15* trying to do before it accidentally crashed on the lunar surface?

26. All in all, how many manned lunar landings have there been? What was the date of the final lunar landing? _____

Early Space Exploration

Make a Time Line

After reading pages 6–24, you should have an overall understanding of the early days of space exploration and the race to the moon. It is important to realize that political reasons were as important as scientific reasons to explore space and go to the moon. It is difficult to imagine reaching the moon at the speed it was reached without taking into account the political issues of the day. Seeing a time line of events helps students put the political and scientific achievements into relative perspective. Furthermore, this is a wonderful integration of science and social science curricula.

In this activity, you and your students will create a time line of events beginning in 1957 with the launch of the Soviet Union's *Sputnik* and culminating in 1969 with the first manned moon landing of *Apollo 11*. In only 12 years, the world went from putting a satellite in orbit to landing men on the surface of the moon! These 12 years may be the greatest period of accelerated technological achievement ever seen on Earth. In 1999 we will celebrate the 30th anniversary of the first lunar landing.

In order to make a time line, you will need to allow for equal spacing between the years 1957 and 1969 and enough room to record important events. A 12-foot time line would allow one foot for each year. Divide each foot into inches to make note of the months of the year. (There are 12 inches in a foot and 12 months in a year—a happy coincidence!)

Students should illustrate the time line with the drawings included in this book or drawings of their own creation to represent important events during this period. You may wish to use the time line of events on page 5 as a guide for the important events. Further, your students may also wish to do some research into some of the other issues occurring between 1957 and 1969. You might wish to team up with your school's social studies teacher for this part. For example, the Vietnam War also played a role in the continuing Cold War between the United States and Soviet Union and added to the fever pitch of the space race.

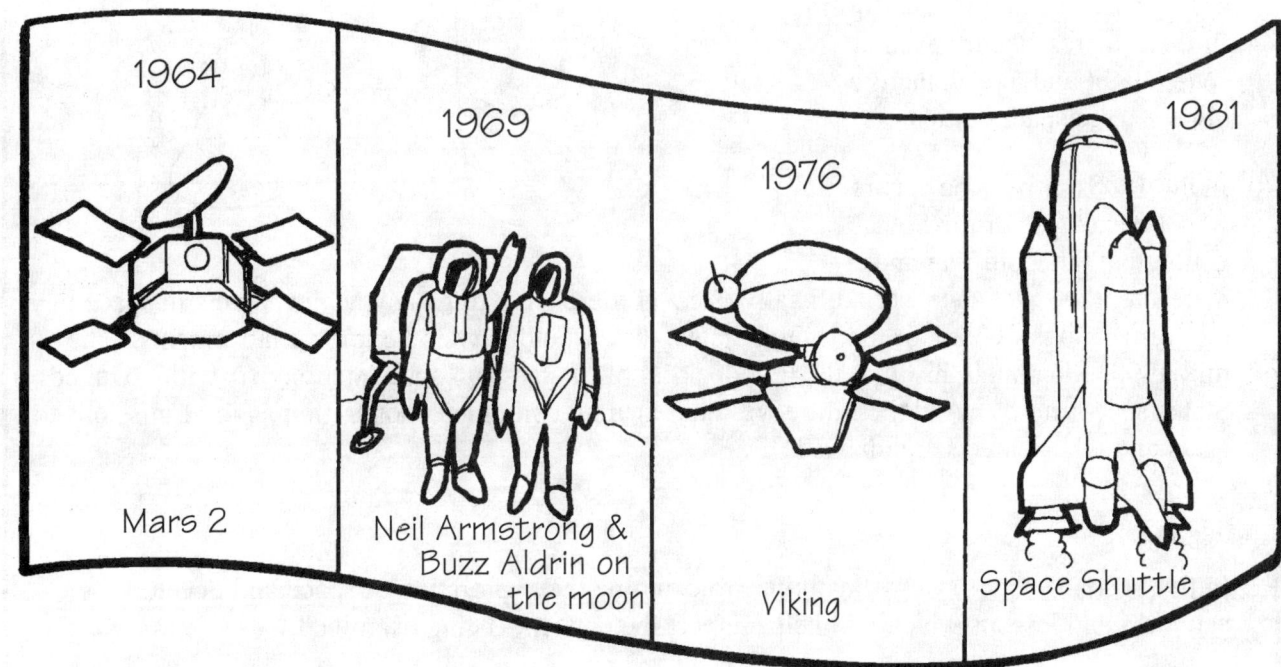

Post-Lunar Landing Space Exploration

Important Events: 1969–1997

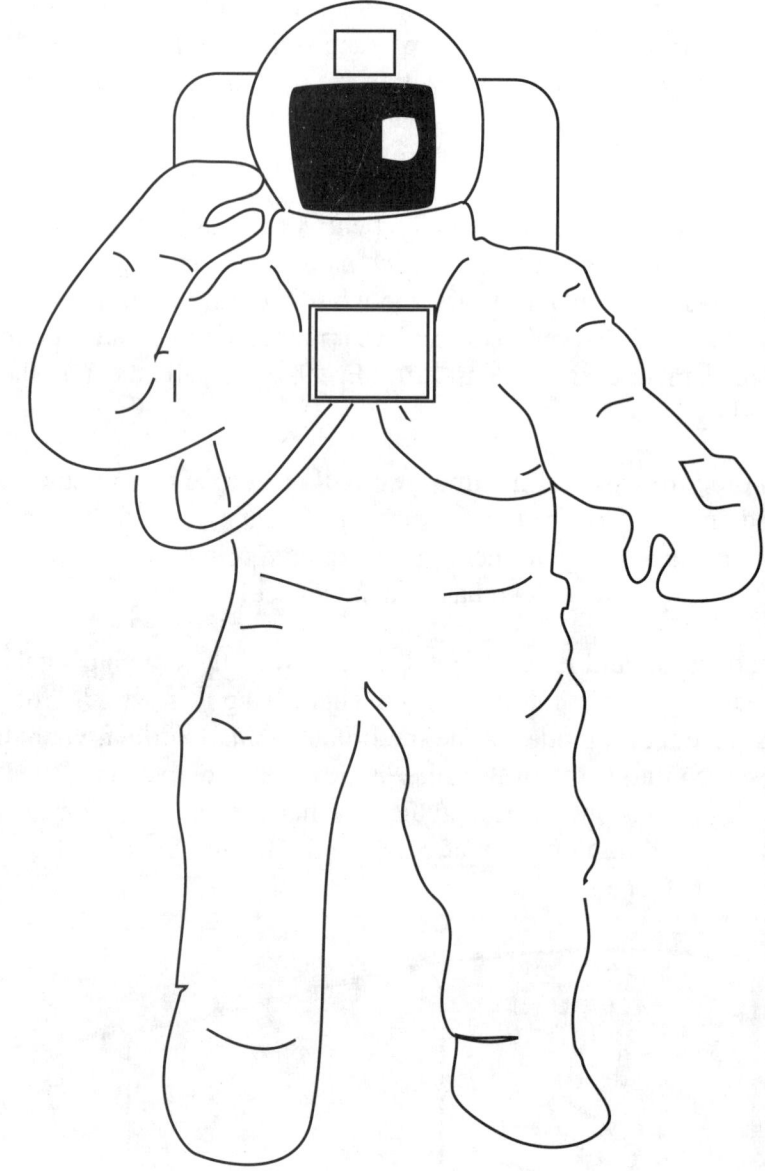

With the landing of *Apollo 17* back on Earth on December 17, 1972, NASA ended the *Apollo* Lunar Landing program. The nation had lost interest in the moon, and the federal funding had been slashed. Much of the country felt that if America had already won the race to the moon, why should we continue to go back? Domestic problems at home—the Vietnam War, homelessness, and other world events—dominated the public's concerns.

Expensive manned missions to the moon had to come to an end. Following the moon landings, both the Soviet Union and United States turned their attention to space matters closer to home. Both countries began experimenting with Earth-orbiting space stations, and in 1980, the United States launched the first re-usable space shuttle in an effort to further its presence in manned space flight and to eventually build a large space station.

In the 1990s, it became apparent with the collapse of the Soviet Union that the Cold War and, therefore, the space race were officially over. If there were to be any achievements in space by the former Soviet Union or the United States, they would have to be joint achievements. The mid-1990s illustrated this with the first docking of the Russian space station *Mir* with a United States space shuttle. And the future will demonstrate continued cooperation as joint missions to Mars and other planets are planned.

◆ ◆ ◆

In this second section, we will continue to examine the exploration of space and develop activities and lessons which will help support the concepts being examined.

Post-Lunar Landing Space Exploration

Important Events: 1969–1997 *(cont.)*

Date	Events
4/19/71	Soviet Union launches *Salyut 1*, first Earth-orbiting space station.
3/3/72	United States launches *Pioneer 10* to Jupiter (arrives 12/3/73).
12/7/72	*Apollo 17* leaves lunar surface. Schmitt and Cernan become the last men to walk on the moon.
4/6/73	United States launches *Pioneer 11* to Jupiter and Saturn.
5/14/73	United States launches its first Earth-orbiting space station, *Skylab*.
7/17/75	*Apollo* and *Soyuz* spacecraft link up, first joint U.S.-Soviet space mission.
8/20/75	*Viking 1* spacecraft and lander is launched to Mars (arrives 7/20/76).
9/9/75	*Viking 2* spacecraft and lander is launched to Mars (arrives 9/3/76).
8/20/77	United States launches *Voyager 2* to Jupiter, Saturn, Uranus, and Neptune.
9/5/77	United States launches *Voyager 1* to Jupiter and Saturn.
4/12/81	United States launches space shuttle *Columbia* on its maiden voyage.
6/13/83	*Pioneer 10* becomes first man-made object to leave the solar system.
1/86	*Voyager 2* reaches Uranus.
1/28/86	Space shuttle *Challenger* explodes 73 seconds after takeoff. Nation mourns the loss of seven astronauts. Shuttle program is grounded.
2/20/86	Soviet Union launches the Core module to the space station *Mir*.
3/13/86	Soviet Union sends first people to occupy *Mir* space station.
9/29/88	Space shuttle *Discovery* puts America back in space!
5/4/89	*Magellan* spacecraft to Venus is launched (arrives 8/10/90).
8/89	*Voyager 2* reaches Neptune.
10/12/89	*Galileo* spacecraft and probe to Jupiter launched (probe arrives 12/7/95).
6/94	Space shuttle *Endeavor* becomes first U.S. shuttle to link with Russian *Mir* space station, first joint U.S.-Russian mission since 1975.
11/7/96	*Global Surveyor* spacecraft is launched to Mars (arrives 9/12/97).
12/4/96	*Pathfinder* spacecraft and rover are launched to Mars (arrive 7/4/97).
10/15/97	*Cassini* spacecraft to Saturn is launched (will arrive in 2004?).

Post-Lunar Landing Space Exploration

Space Stations

Salyut http://www.nauts.com/histpace/vehicles/histsalyut.html

Soon after *Apollo 11* touched down on the moon's surface in 1969, the Soviet Union closed their manned lunar space program. Next on their agenda was to launch a permanent space station in orbit around Earth. They accomplished this with the launch of the *Salyut* space station on April 19, 1971. *Salyut 1* was occupied only once by a group of three Russian cosmonauts. They arrived at the space station on June 6, 1971, and stayed until June 29. Sadly, when the cosmonauts came back to the Earth aboard their *Soyuz* spacecraft, they experienced a loss of air pressure in their capsule during re-entry and were killed. The *Salyut 1* space station, however, remained in orbit until it fell back to Earth on May 28, 1973.

The idea behind the *Salyut* space station was to create a permanent base in space to understand the long-term effects of weightlessness on the body and to study the sun and other astronomical bodies. With the *Salyut* program, the Soviets held the world record for the number of manned continuous days in space.

All in all, the Soviet Union would launch six *Salyut*-class space stations into orbit. Each one, except *Salyut 7* (the sixth *Salyut* to be launched—in 1982), has since come back to Earth. Space stations with orbits very close to Earth will ultimately fall back to Earth due to the pull of gravity and the drag created by skimming the outer atmosphere (see the text activities on pages 33–35 for a demonstration of why this occurs). While *Salyut 7* still orbits the Earth, it has been uninhabited since 1984. The *Salyut* space station program would ultimately be replaced with the *Mir* space station launched in 1986.

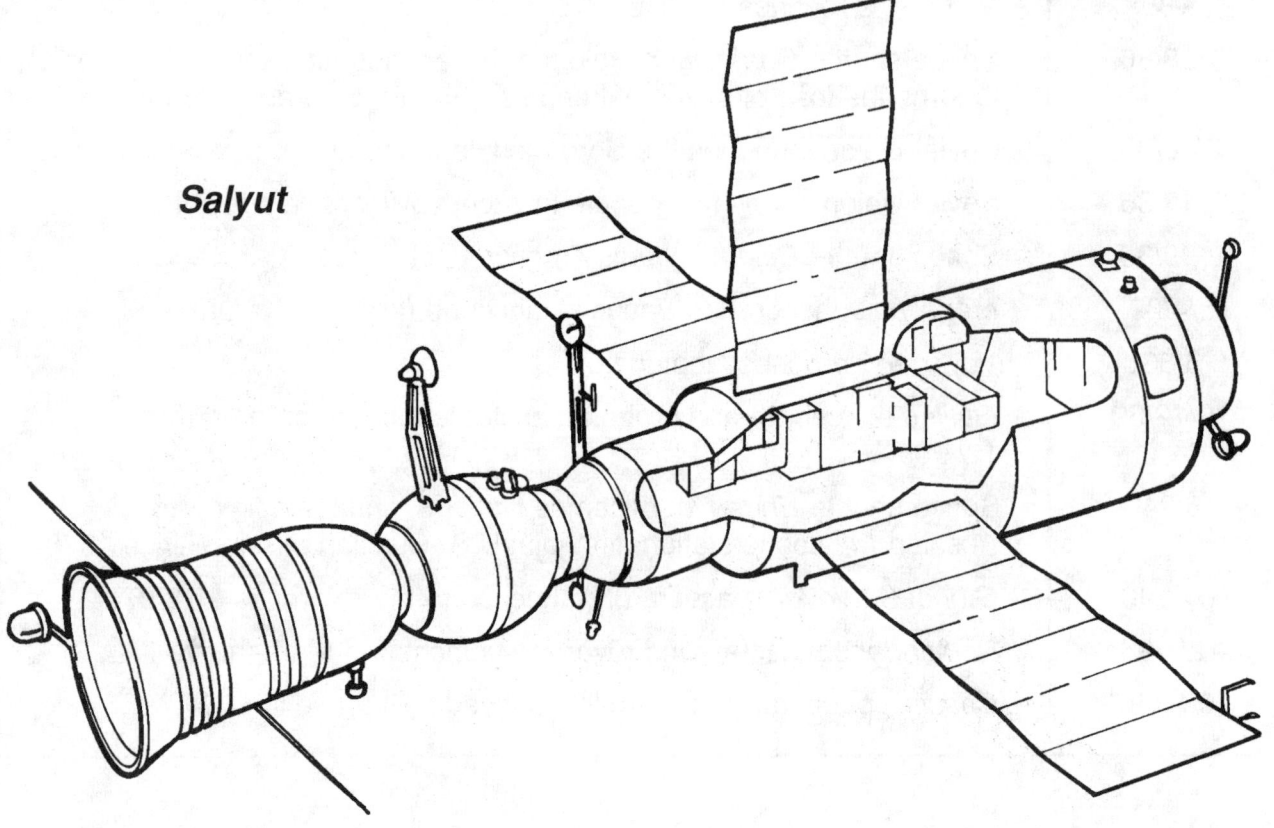

Salyut

Post-Lunar Landing Space Exploration

Space Stations *(cont.)*

Skylab http://www.ksc.nasa.gov/history/skylab/skylab.html

Skylab was launched on May 14, 1973, in an effort to place a permanent American space station in orbit around Earth. Like the Soviet's *Salyut* program, *Skylab* was designed to test man's endurance on long space missions as well as to explore astronomical phenomena in a way not possible on the ground.

Skylab itself was fashioned from an empty third-stage booster rocket of a Saturn V rocket (the same rockets that put project *Apollo* on the moon in the late '60s and early '70s). Astronaut crews would reach *Skylab* in an *Apollo* space capsule aboard a modified Saturn V rocket.

During the launch of *Skylab*, the meteoroid deflection shield accidentally came apart and left a hole in the side of the space station. This needed to be repaired by the first astronauts to live aboard *Skylab*. They placed a gold foil shield over the hole to protect them from the burning rays of the sun.

Skylab was visited by a total of nine astronauts on a series of three missions in 1973. During their visits, the astronauts conducted experiments on solar activity and human endurance in space and made observations of Comet Kohoutek.

In the mid 1970s, greater than expected solar activity caused *Skylab* to slow down in its orbit. On July 11, 1979, *Skylab's* orbit finally brought it close enough to Earth that it re-entered the atmosphere and impacted on Earth's surface. Much of the debris landed in the Indian Ocean, but some parts landed in a sparsely populated section of western Australia. *Skylab* has so far been America's one and only space station.

Space Station *Skylab*: 1973–1974

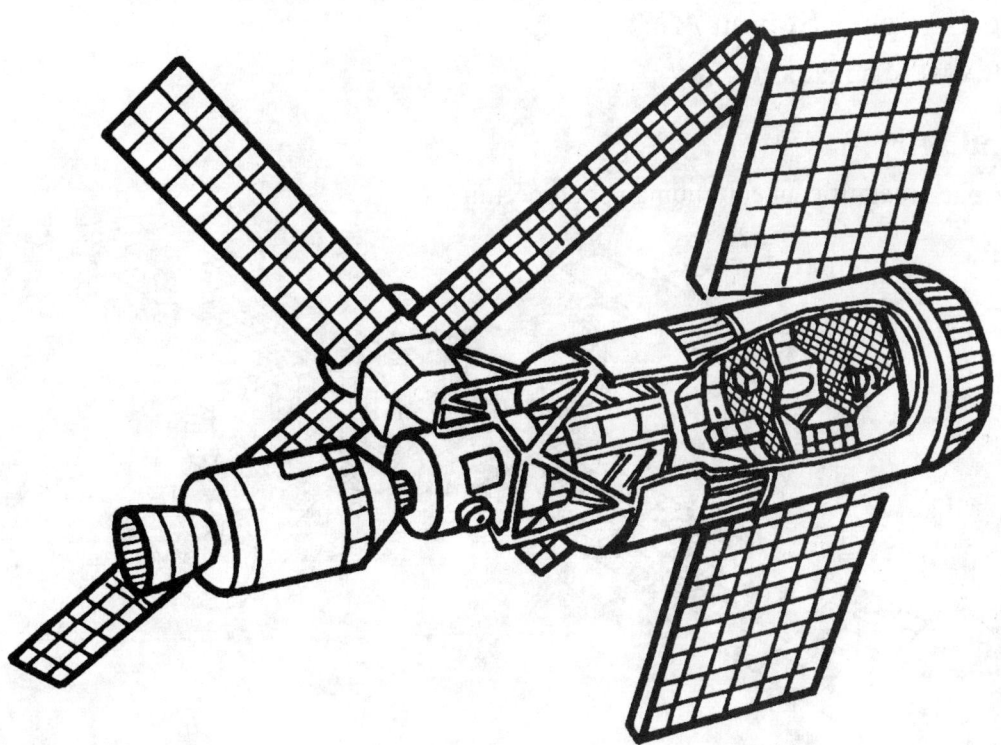

Post-Lunar Landing Space Exploration

Space Stations *(cont.)*

Mir

The Core module of the *Mir* space station was launched by the Soviet Union on February 20, 1986, and was designed to be operational for seven years. In February 1998 *Mir* marked its 12th year in orbit! Loosely translated, *Mir* means "peace" in Russian, and it was the idea of the designers that *Mir* would be a modular space station to which additional pieces could be added later. Currently, *Mir* has four modules connected to its core, and an additional module connected to one of the four. The additional module is known as the *Spektr Module* (launched in 1995), the most recent addition to the station.

Throughout its 12-year history, *Mir* has been occupied about 90% of the time. Two- and three-person crews arrive at the station in a *Soyuz* spacecraft and dock at one end. While this docking is occurring, the crew currently stationed on board will put on their spacesuits and enter the *Soyuz* spacecraft they came in, which is docked at another port. This is done for safety in case an emergency arises during docking. When docking is complete, both crews meet in the main core of *Mir*. After a debriefing, the old crew will leave in the *Soyuz* they arrived in, leaving the new crew on board *Mir*.

On June 26, 1995, the United States' space shuttle *Atlantis* became the first American craft to dock with the Russian space station. An exchange of passengers occurred, and American astronaut Norman Thagard boarded *Atlantis* after having lived on *Mir* for 115 days. Thagard had been the first American to ride aboard a *Soyuz* rocket and the first American to live aboard the space station *Mir*. The arrival of Americans on *Mir* demonstrated a new spirit of cooperation between the two superpowers.

Recently, the *Mir* space station has been in the news a number of times for the problems it has been having in space. The aging spacecraft has been plagued with such problems as a fire in an oxygen tank and a collision with a docking *Soyuz* rocket. For the latest information about the space station *Mir*, check out the following Web sites:

ISS Phase 1—Space Station *Mir*

http://www.osf.hq.nasa.gov/mir/

Shuttle and *Mir*:

http://space.magnificent.com/human/shuttle&mir

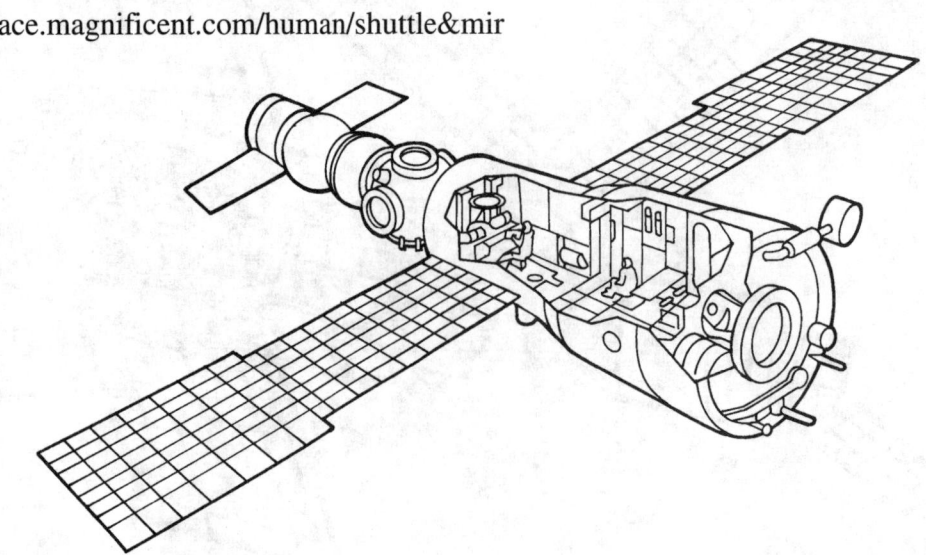

Post-Lunar Landing Space Exploration

Activity #5: Understanding Orbits

Materials
- tetherball on a rope

Procedure
1. Ask a student to hold the end of the tetherball rope and swing the ball around himself or herself in a circle.
2. With everyone standing clear of the student holding the rope, ask the student to suddenly let go of the rope and watch where the ball goes.

Discussion
When an object like a space station is placed in orbit around a planet such as Earth, it is kept in orbit by the pull of gravity from the planet. If the planet were to suddenly disappear, the space station would fly off into space in a straight line. In this activity, you swung a tetherball around and around in a circle before letting it go. You represented Earth, and the rope represented the gravitational attraction between Earth and a space station (the ball). No one is quite sure what gravity is, but the rope is an effective illustration of the attractive properties of gravity. Large objects (such as Earth) have a great "pulling" effect on smaller objects (such as *Skylab* or the space shuttle).

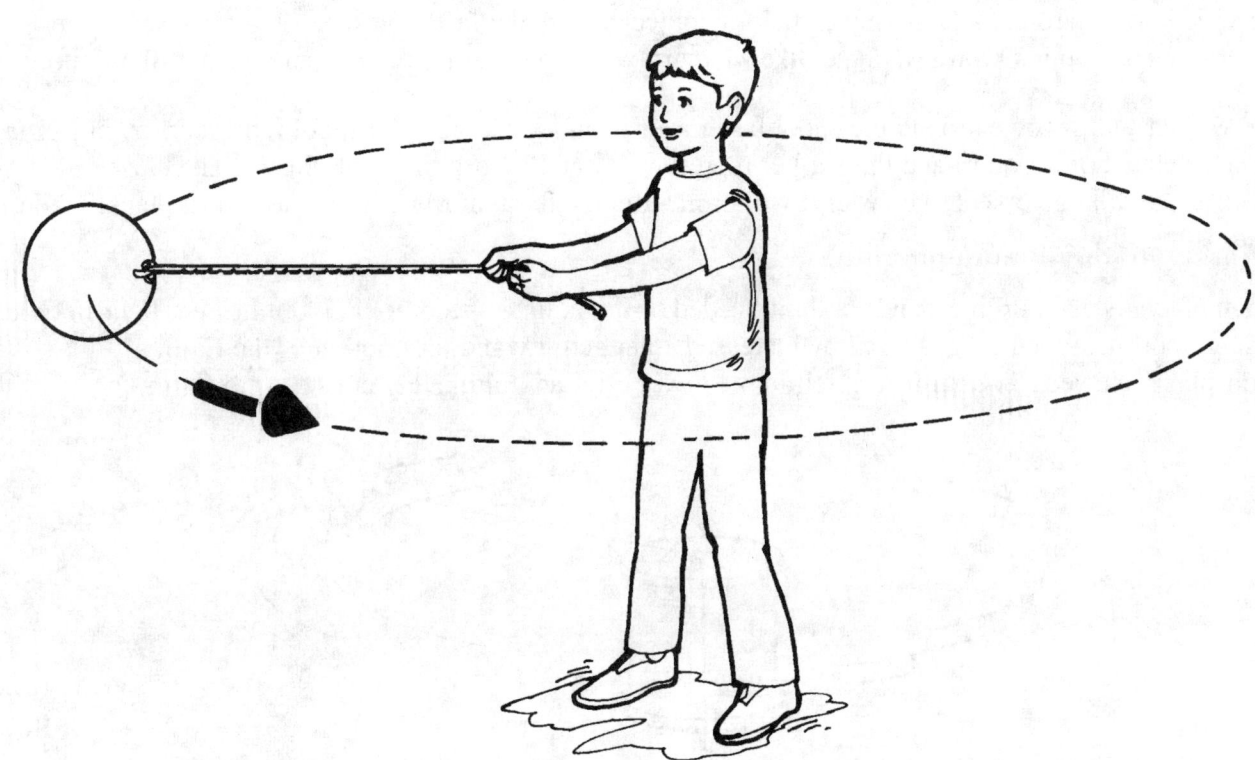

Post-Lunar Landing Space Exploration

Activity #6: Understanding Orbits II

Materials

- spool of thread
- washer

Procedure

1. Thread a length of string or thread through the spool. Three feet (one meter) long is enough.
2. Tie the washer to one end of the string and hold onto the other end of the string.
3. Hold the spool in one hand and the end of the string in the other hand.
4. Begin to swing the spool in a circular motion so that the washer revolves around the spool in a giant circle.
5. As the washer revolves around the spool, slowly pull the string through the spool with your other hand.

Discussion

No one is exactly certain how gravity works; not even our top scientists claim to understand it. However, we can do some amazing things! One of the known properties of gravity is that when a tiny object is in orbit around a large object, the tiny object will make faster orbits as it gets closer to the larger object. In other words, a planet like Mercury will orbit the sun faster than a planet like Pluto.

The washer will revolve around the spool faster as it is pulled closer. The spool represents an object in space (a planet or the sun), and the washer represents a satellite orbiting that object. The closer a satellite is to a large object, the faster it will orbit. Remember that Mercury is the fastest planet while Pluto is the slowest.

When *Skylab* was in orbit around Earth, it needed to maintain a speed of 17,500 miles per hour in order to stay in orbit. When drag, caused by increased solar activity and the friction of the Earth's atmosphere, slowed *Skylab* down, it fell into a lower orbit and ultimately crashed into Earth.

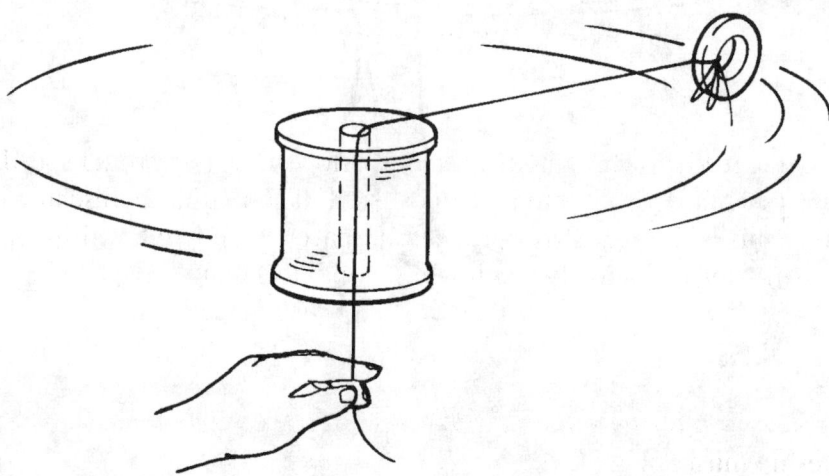

Post-Lunar Landing Space Exploration

Activity #7: Understanding Orbits III

Materials
- large sewing hoop
- tulle (fine "netting" available at fabric stores)
- tennis ball
- marble
- four chairs

Procedure
1. Stretch the tulle across the large sewing hoop so that it is just fairly snug. It should be somewhat loose, but more snug than loose.
2. Place the sewing hoop in the center of four chairs arranged facing each other to support the sewing hoop.
3. Place the tennis ball in the center of the sewing hoop. This will put a depression in the tulle.
4. Quickly roll a marble along the outer edge of the tulle so that it "orbits" the tennis ball. Notice how long it takes before the marble finally hits the tennis ball.
5. Repeat step 4, but this time roll the marble at a slower speed. Notice that the marble will hit the tennis ball in a shorter period of time than it did before.

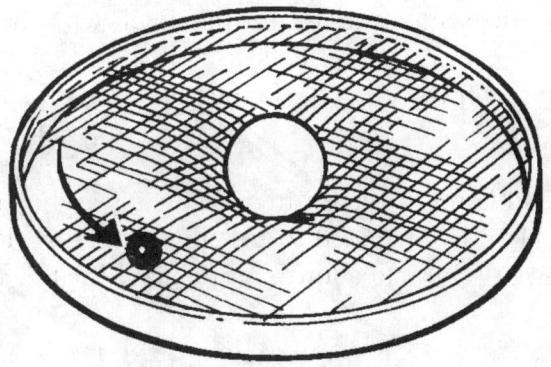

Discussion
When the space shuttle is ready to come home, it merely slows down its orbital speed of close to 17,500 miles per hour and "falls" back into the atmosphere. The Earth, (represented in this demonstration as the tennis ball) creates a depression in space, much like a whirlpool creates a depression in water. Any object flying by Earth will fall into this depression and be swirled around Earth like an object in a whirlpool. If an object such as a space station or the space shuttle were to maintain a speed of over 17,500 miles per hour, it would overcome the pull of the Earth's gravity and remain in orbit around Earth. But, if it slows down, the gravity of Earth and the friction created by skimming the top of the atmosphere will pull the spacecraft back to the surface. As the old saying observes: "What goes up must come down."

© Teacher Created Materials, Inc.   35   #2383 Exploring Mars and Beyond—Challenging

Post-Lunar Landing Space Exploration

Vomit Comet: Understanding Free-Fall

KC-135, Zero Gravity Trainer   http://zeta.lerc.nasa.gov/kjenks/kc-135.html

Have you ever wondered how astronauts train for the weightlessness they will experience in space? No, there isn't an "anti-gravity" room at NASA. Instead, the astronauts experience "free-fall" aboard an airplane nicknamed the *Vomit Comet*. The astronauts fly aboard this modified Boeing 707 airplane at a steep climbing angle and then drop suddenly for several hundred feet. While the airplane drops, the passengers experience a few seconds of weightlessness.

The general flight pattern involves leveling off at around 26,000 feet and then pulling the nose of the plane up in a steep 45 degree climb to 36,000 feet. Once 36,000 feet is reached, the pilot then noses the plane down, and several seconds of weightlessness can be felt until the plane again levels off at 26,000 feet. During one flight, astronauts will experience between 40 and 100 parabolic arcs of weightlessness!

It is also interesting to note that in order to provide a sense of realism to the movie *Apollo 13*, the cast and crew filmed the space scenes on a set built inside a KC-135 trainer. They spent over six months flying up and down to film the exciting sequences.

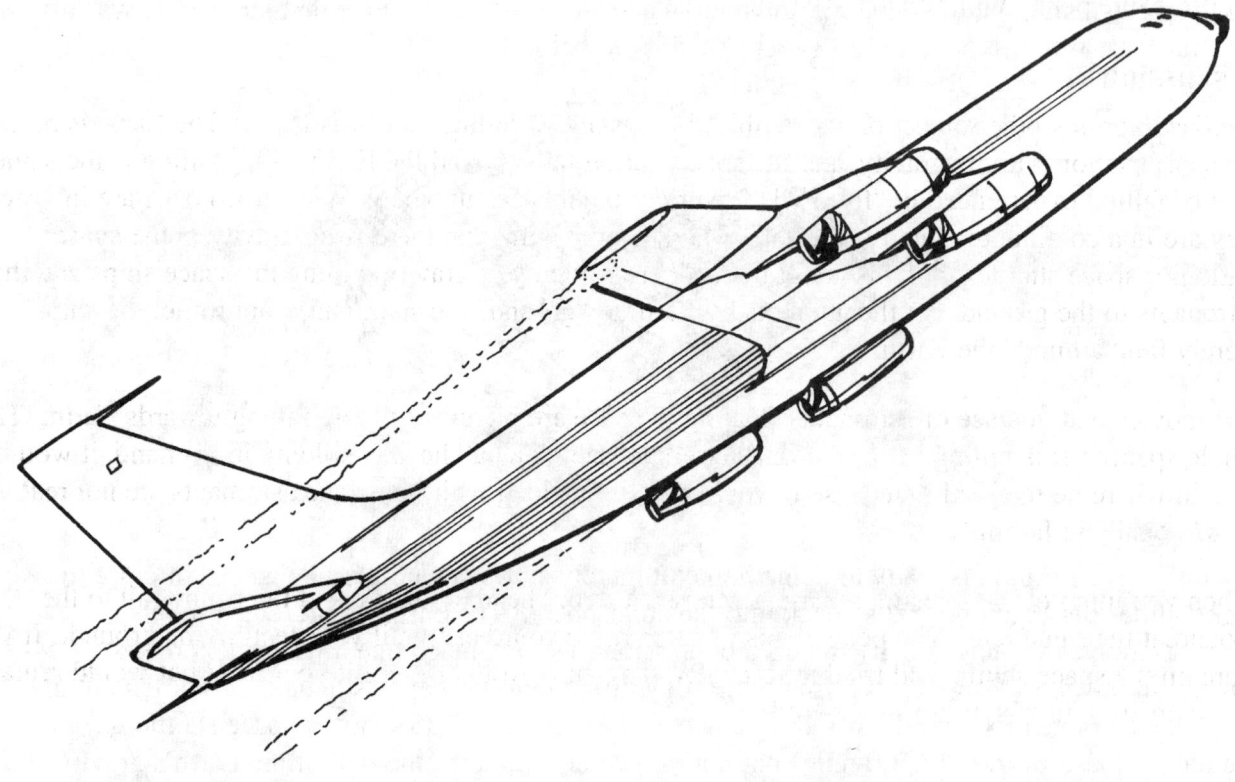

Post-Lunar Landing Space Exploration

Activity #8: Understanding Free-Fall

Materials
- penny
- table (sturdy enough to stand upon)

Procedure

> **Caution: This activity is to be done only with adult supervision!**

1. Ask one student to stand on top of a sturdy table with a penny in her or his hand.
2. Ask the student to extend an arm high above her or his head with the penny in that hand.
3. On a count of three, ask the student to jump off the table to the floor and release the penny above her or his head at the same time. When the feet leave the table is when the penny should be released. (This may take several attempts to get the coordination of events correct.)

Results

The penny should strike the top of the head only after he or she lands on the ground. While the student is falling, the penny will remain above his or her head.

Discussion

As *Skylab* or any other object orbits Earth, it is constantly "falling" towards Earth. The Earth is pulling the space station with its gravity, and the space station falls around the Earth. This falling is the same type of falling experienced in "free-fall" type rides at amusement parks. When astronauts are in space, they are in a continuous state of free-fall. Many people think that there is no gravity in the space station or space shuttles, but this is not true. There is plenty of gravity pulling the space ships and the astronauts to the ground, but the attempts by Earth to "ground" the space ships are futile; the ships merely fall "around" the Earth.

The movies that you see of astronauts floating in space are pictures of them falling towards Earth. The whole spacecraft is falling. If an astronaut were to release a ball he was holding in his hand, it would remain where he released it because it would be falling along with him. The astronauts are not really floating; they're falling!

When you jump off a table and release a penny over your head, both you and the penny fall to the ground at the same rate. The penny doesn't catch up to your head until your feet hit the ground. If you were on the space shuttle and tried this activity, the penny would never hit your head but would remain in the position in which it was released.

Post-Lunar Landing Space Exploration

Space Shuttle

Space Shuttle http://shuttle.nasa.gov

Launched for the first time on April 12, 1981, the space shuttle *Columbia* put Americans back in space for the first time in six years. John Young (Commander of the *Apollo 16* Lunar Landing mission) and rookie Astronaut Robert Crippen took *Columbia* up for her maiden voyage. The last time Americans had flown in space was in July 1975 on the first joint United States-Soviet Union *Apollo-Soyuz* mission.

The chief mission of the space shuttle is to create a re-usable space vehicle capable of building a permanent space station in orbit around Earth. To date, plans for the space station, known as *Freedom*, have fallen far behind schedule, and the shuttle has served other purposes. For example, the space shuttle has been instrumental in launching a number of communications and astronomical satellites such as the Hubble Space Telescope and the *Galileo* probe which went on to Jupiter. And, in joint efforts with the former Soviet Union, the space shuttle has begun to fulfill its original mission as a carrier of passengers to and from the space station *Mir*. On June 29, 1995, the 100th space shuttle mission, STS-71, became the first United States space shuttle to dock with the Russian *Mir* space station. Since then, a number of space shuttles have docked with *Mir*.

Facts About the Space Shuttle

In order to orbit Earth, the space shuttle (or any other spaceship) must travel at speeds of about 17,500 miles per hour (28,000 kilometers per hour).

The space shuttle flies between 190 to 330 miles (300 to 530 km) above sea level. Major airliners fly between five to six miles above sea level.

The shuttle's large external tank contains over 500,000 gallons of liquid oxygen and liquid hydrogen which are burned through the shuttle's three main engines.

First Space Shuttle Launch—April 12, 1981

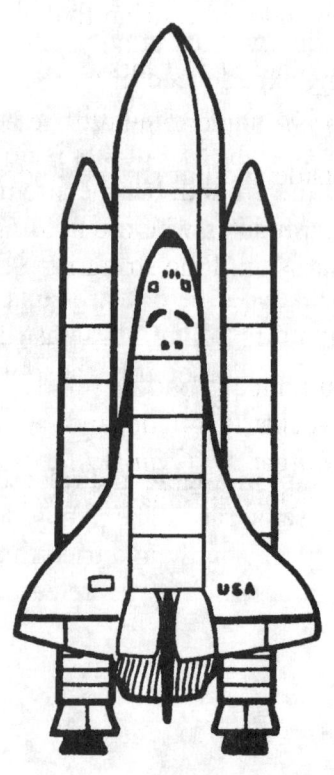

Post-Lunar Landing Space Exploration

Activity #9: How Big Are Space Ships?

Now that you have some background into the different kinds of manned spacecraft launched into space, the following activity will give you some idea of the relative dimensions of these crafts.

Materials

- photocopy of page 40
- heavy cardstock (Index cards will work fine.)
- glue
- toilet paper rolls
- hole punch
- string
- pencil

Procedure

1. Photocopy page 40 and cut out the cards.
2. Glue the cards to heavy cardstock.
3. Use the hole punch to punch a hole in the top of the card where indicated.
4. Use the hole punch to punch a hole in the side of nine toilet paper rolls.
5. Measure out the length of string indicated on each card by "Rocket Length."
6. Tie one end of the string to the hole in the toilet paper roll and wrap it around the roll.
7. Tie the other end of the string around the hole in the card.
8. Assign one student to hold the toilet paper roll and another to hold the card.
9. Go outside and line up the students who are holding the card against a wall or a fence.
10. Ask the students who are holding the toilet paper rolls to insert a pencil in the rolls and walk backwards until the string is fully extended.

Discussion

What do you notice about the relative sizes of the rockets? Which country seemed to build longer rockets? Is rocket length dependent upon the rocket's purpose? (*Yes, when a rocket goes to the moon, it needs to be longer so it can hold more fuel*). What do you notice about the amount of living space each capsule had? Do you think there was a lot of room to move around in some of the earlier space capsules?

© Teacher Created Materials, Inc.　　　　　　39　　　　　　#2383 Exploring Mars and Beyond—Challenging

Post-Lunar Landing Space Exploration

Activity #9: How Big Are Space Ships? *(cont.)*

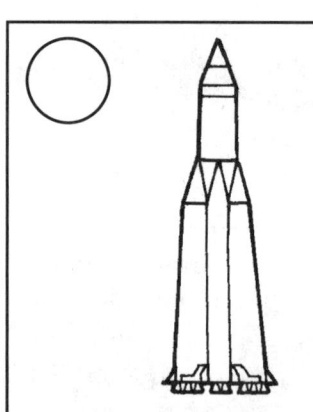

Vostok
Rocket Length: 38.4 m
Capsule Length: 5.0 m

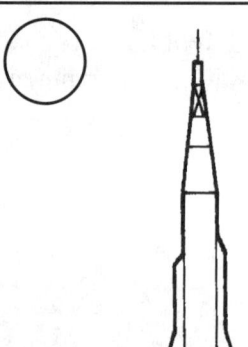

Mercury
Rocket Length: 21.9 m
Capsule Length: 3.3 m

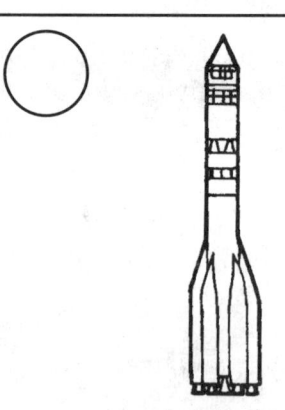

Voskhod
Rocket Length: 44.3 m
Capsule Length: 7.1 m

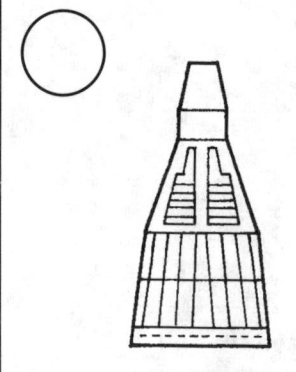

Gemini
Rocket Length: 33.2 m
Capsule Length: 5.8 m

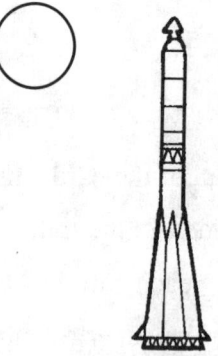

Soyuz
Rocket Length: 39.3
Capsule Length: 7.1 m

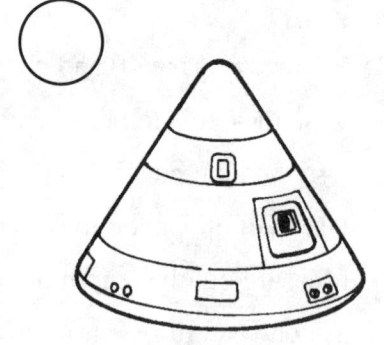

Apollo
Rocket Length: 111 m
Capsule Length: 10.5 m

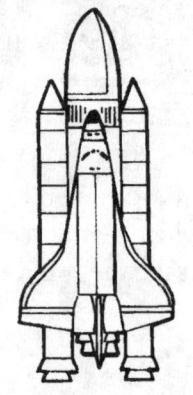

Space Shuttle
Shuttle Length: 37.0 m
Crew Compartment Dimensions:
2.7 x 4.0 x 3.7 m

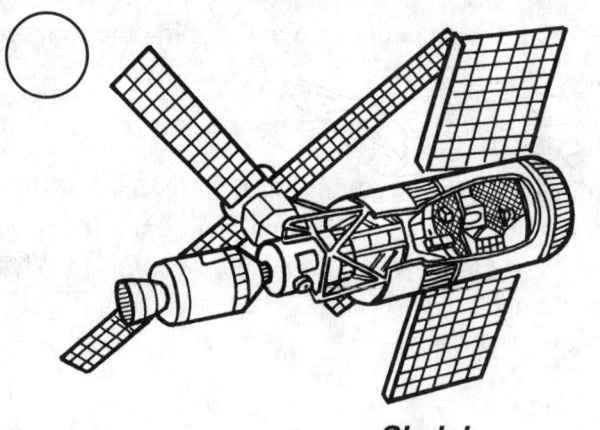

Skylab
Length: 36 m
Diameter: 6.4 m

Unmanned Missions to the Planets

Pioneer

Pioneer http://nssdc.gsfc.nasa.gov/planetary

The principal missions of *Pioneers 10* and *11* were to explore the planets of the outer solar system. Launched on March 3, 1972, *Pioneer 10* became the first unmanned spaceship to reach Jupiter on December 3, 1973. *Pioneer 11*, launched on April 6, 1973, followed its sister ship to Jupiter and became the first spaceship to reach Saturn. While operating around Jupiter, it took over 46 minutes for the *Pioneer* images and data to travel at the speed of light across space and back to Earth!

To the astonished amazement of NASA scientists, *Pioneer 10* continues to transmit data back to Earth to this day, even though the spacecraft is almost 70 Astronomical Units from the sun! (One Astronomical Unit is the distance from Earth to the sun—about 93 million miles. *Pioneer 10* is almost 70 times that distance away.) In fact, *Pioneer 10* has outlived the money which funds its mission. As of March 31, 1997, for lack of funding NASA stopped following the spacecraft's activity.

On June 13, 1983, *Pioneer 10* became the first spacecraft ever to leave our solar system. Attached to *Pioneer 10* is a plaque which depicts the drawing of a man and a woman as well as a drawing of our solar system. Someday, perhaps, the spacecraft may be found by other travelers trying to find signs of life in the universe.

Pioneer

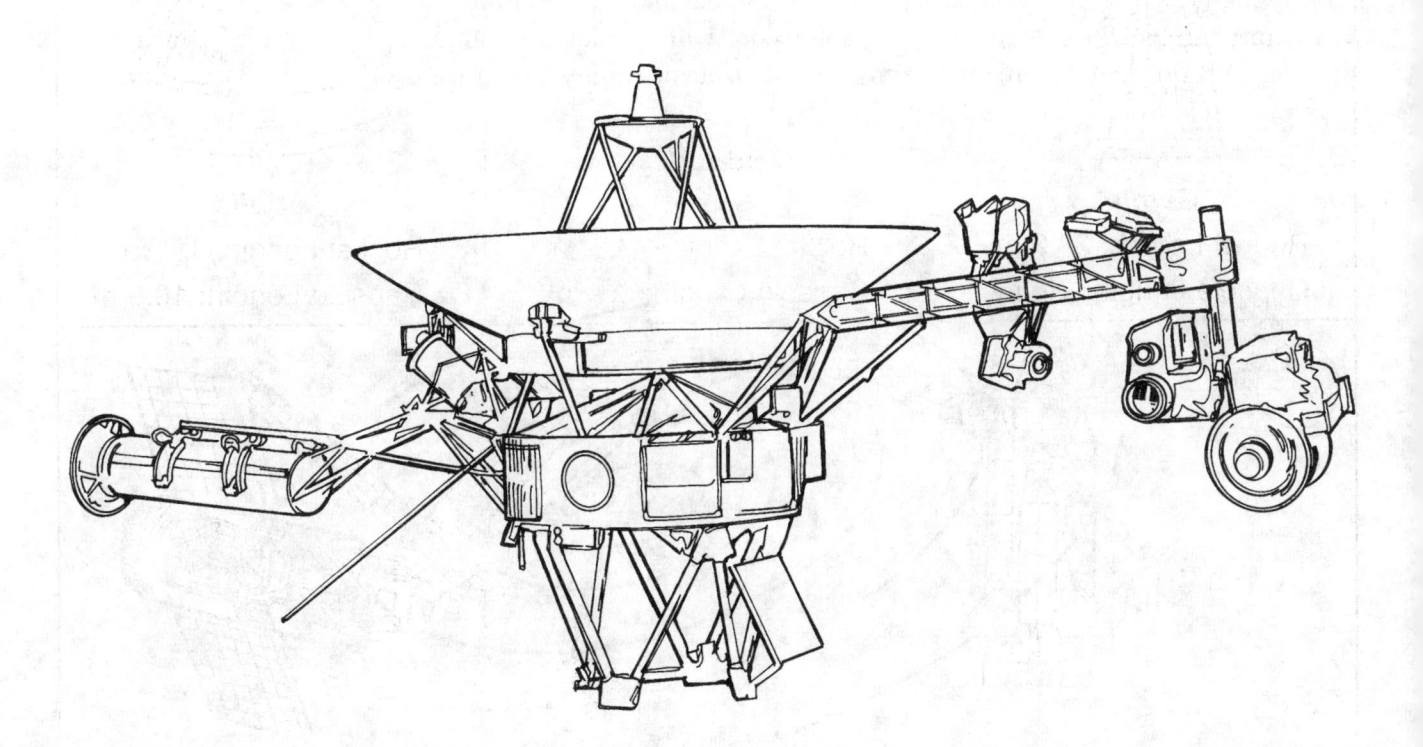

© *Teacher Created Materials, Inc.* 41 #2383 *Exploring Mars and Beyond—Challenging*

Unmanned Missions to the Planets

Voyager

Voyager http://nssdc.gsfc.nasa.gov/planetary

To date, the *Voyager* missions of the late 1970s and early 1980s remain our most recent and best view of the planets in our outer solar system. *Voyager 2* was launched on August 20, 1977, and was followed a few days later by *Voyager 1* on September 5, 1977. While *Voyager 2* was launched first, its trajectory (path) to Jupiter would make it arrive after *Voyager 1*.

Voyager 1 arrived at Jupiter in March 1979 while *Voyager 2* arrived in July 1979. At Jupiter, the Voyagers discovered a ring around the planet, three more moons, and confirmed volcanic activity on one of Jupiter's moons—Io, the only body in the solar system, besides Earth, to have confirmed active volcanoes. Following their discoveries at Jupiter, *Voyagers 1* and *2* moved on to Saturn. *Voyager 1* arrived in November 1980 while *Voyager 2* followed in August 1981. While there, the *Voyagers* took the most detailed photographs we have today of the famously ringed planet, discovered three more moons, and discovered that one of Saturn's moons, Triton, has an active atmosphere.

Because of the unique positions of the planets in their orbit around the sun when *Voyager 2* was launched, it was possible to guide *Voyager 2* on a mission to two previously unexplored planets—Uranus and Neptune. *Voyager 2* arrived at Uranus in January 1986 and discovered two new rings and 10 new moons and took a host of photographs of the gaseous planet. In August 1989, *Voyager 2* arrived at Neptune and discovered six moons, photographed Neptune's rings, and discovered on the planet a giant storm called the "great dark spot."

At present, the *Voyager* spacecraft are still operational and are speeding out of our solar system. Each spacecraft carries with it a gold phonograph record which holds the sounds of 60 languages, several musical selections, and a greeting from former President Jimmy Carter (in office at the time of launch).

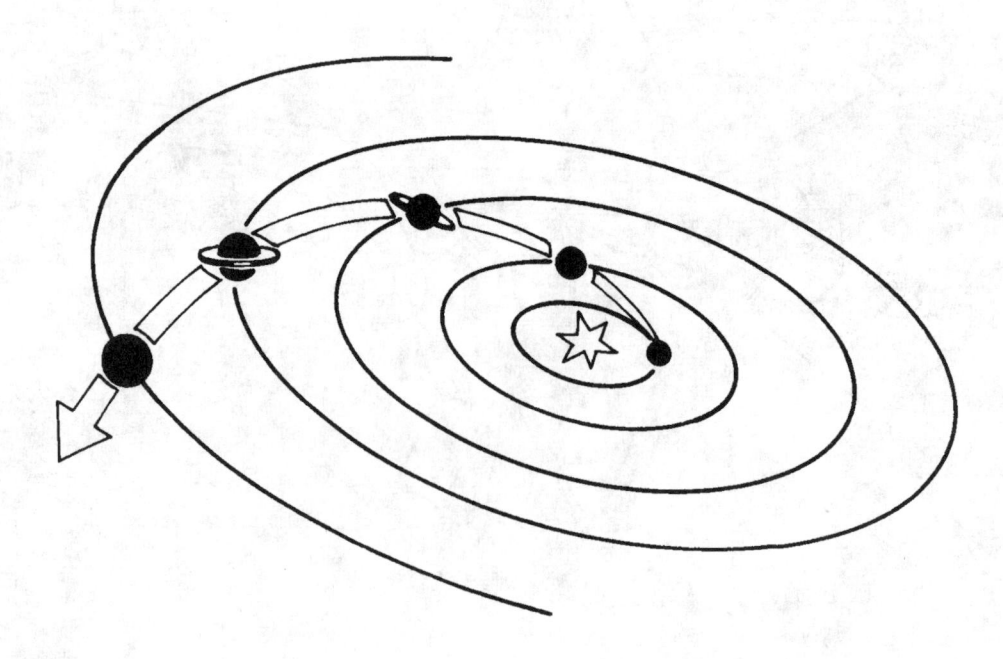

Unmanned Missions to the Planets

Galileo

Galileo http://www.jpl.nasa.gov/galileo

Usually, space probes are launched on top of a booster rocket from Cape Canaveral in Florida, but that was not the case with *Galileo*. Named after the seventeenth-century Italian scientist who discovered Jupiter's moons, the *Galileo* spacecraft was launched from the cargo bay of the space shuttle *Atlantis* on October 12, 1989. From there, *Galileo* was sent on a mission to use the gravity of the inner planets and the sun to help it speed up for its mission to Jupiter. As it gained speed, the spacecraft passed by Earth two times and was even able to make some observations of our moon.

Finally, on July 13, 1995, the *Galileo* spacecraft released a small probe which would enter the atmosphere of Jupiter on December 7, 1995, in order to get an up-close look at the most gigantic planet in our solar system. From data received from the probe, it was discovered that Jupiter contains almost as much helium gas as does our sun (indicating that Jupiter may have been an "almost" star in its earlier stages of development) and that lightning strikes on the planet are over 10 times stronger than they are here on Earth. While the probe was doing its job in the atmosphere of the planet, the *Galileo* mother ship discovered more evidence for the possibility of water beneath the surface of one of Jupiter's moons, Europa, and photographed the collision of Comet Shoemaker-Levy 9, which struck the planet in July 1994. The *Galileo* mother ship became the first spacecraft to go into orbit around the planet Jupiter (the *Pioneers* and *Voyagers* flew by the planet but never orbited), and it continues to relay much information about Jupiter and its moons.

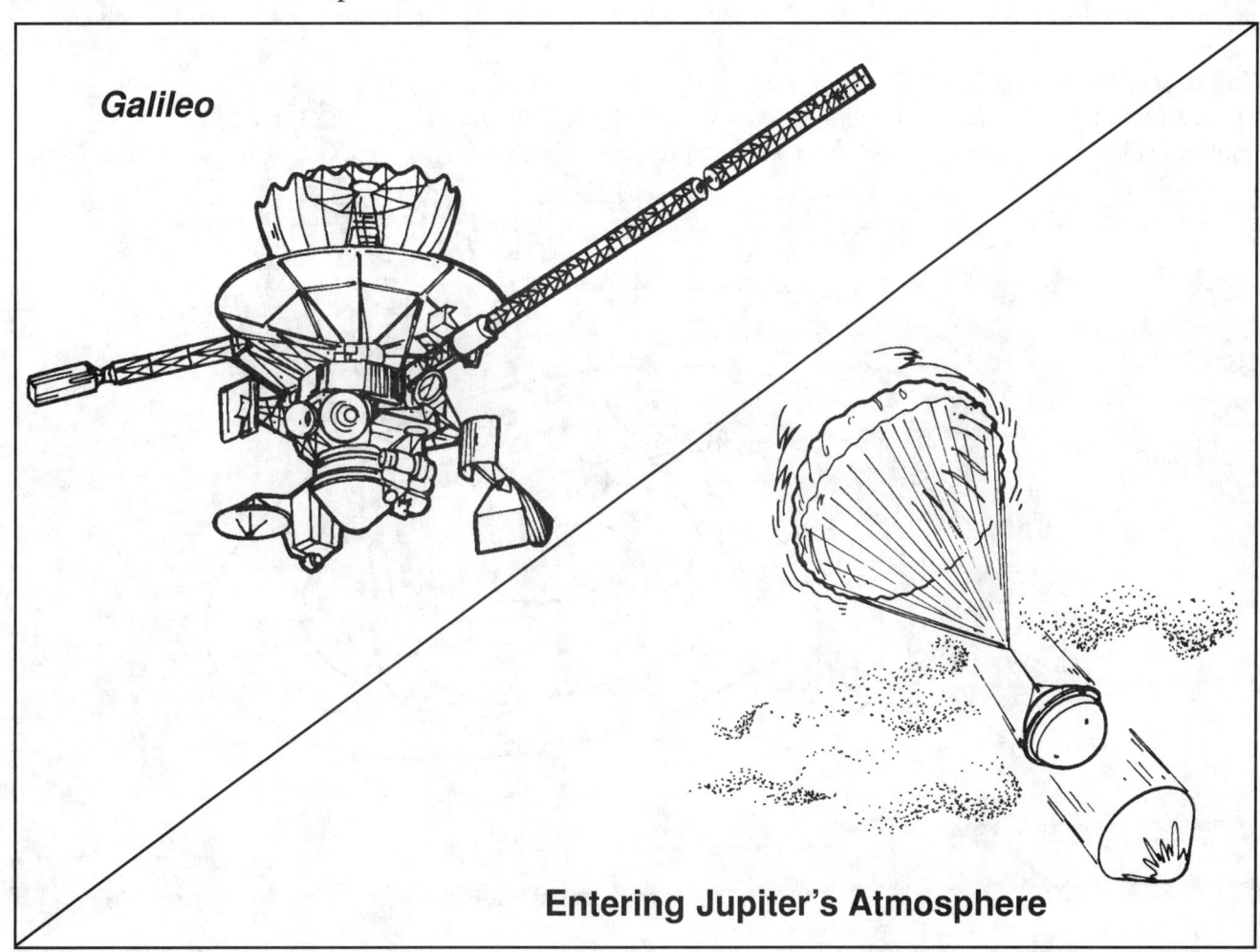

Galileo

Entering Jupiter's Atmosphere

Unmanned Missions to the Planets

Magellan

Magellan http://www.jpl.nasa.gov/magellan

Magellan was launched from the cargo bay of the space shuttle *Atlantis* in May 1989. Its physical design and launch pattern were similar to that of the *Galileo* spacecraft launched in October 1989. Named after the famous sixteenth-century explorer who was the first to circumnavigate the Earth, *Magellan's* mission was to map the surface of the cloud enshrouded planet, Venus.

By August 10, 1990, *Magellan* was in a polar orbit around Venus. By October 12, 1994, *Magellan* had successfully mapped 99% of the planet. NASA ground controllers lost contact with *Magellan* on October 12, but by then it had exceeded its original goal of mapping 70% of the surface.

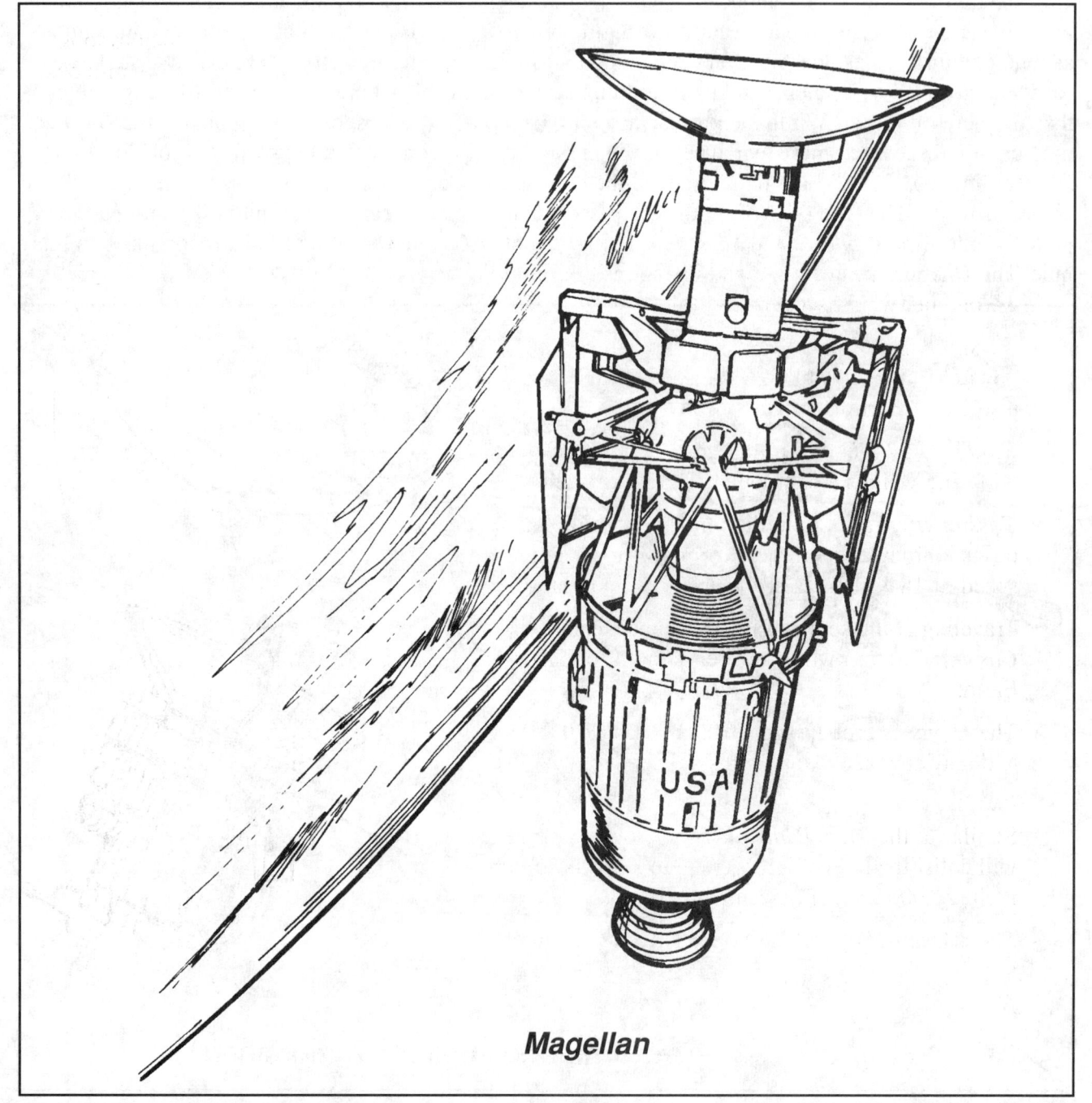

Magellan

Unmanned Missions to the Planets

Cassini

Cassini http://www.jpl.nasa.gov/cassini

On October 15, 1997, NASA launched the $3.4 billion *Cassini* mission to the planet Jupiter. Launched atop a Titan IV-Centaur rocket, *Cassini* will spend seven years traveling to the planet and arrive in the summer of 2004 if all goes well. Once the spacecraft arrives at Saturn, *Cassini* will release the *Huygens* space probe which will land on Titan, the largest of Saturn's 18 moons—and the largest known moon in our solar system.

Prior to launch, the *Cassini* mission was surrounded in a bit of controversy about the 72 pounds (33 kg) of plutonium it carries to power its batteries. Plutonium is a radioactive material which has been used before by NASA to power deep space probes such as *Voyager* and *Galileo* and is feared by some to pose potential health hazards should a rocket explode upon takeoff. Your students may want to look into some of the pros and cons surrounding the use of plutonium in future space exploration missions.

Fascinating Facts About the *Cassini* Mission

- The *Cassini* mission is named after the 17th century astronomer who discovered a gap in Saturn's rings, known today as the Cassini Division.
- The *Huygens* probe is named after the 17th century astronomer who discovered Saturn's rings.
- *Cassini* will first fly towards the sun and use the gravity of the sun and Venus to speed it up. It will also fly by Earth in August 1999.
- *Cassini* is 22 feet (6.7 m) tall and 13 feet (4 m) wide and weighs 4,685 pounds (2,130 kg).
- *Cassini* will travel 2.2 billion miles (3.5 billion km) on its journey and will be traveling at an average speed of 18,720 miles per hour (30,145 km/hr).
- Traveling at the speed of light, a signal sent by *Cassini* at Saturn will take over an hour to reach Earth.
- The *Huygens* probe weighs 700 pounds (320 kg) and may stay active on Titan's surface for four years.
- Similar to the Mars *Pathfinder*, the *Huygens* probe will enlist the help of a parachute to slow its 13,000 mph (21,000 km/hr) descent onto Titan's surface.
- The *Cassini-Huygens* mission is NASA's costliest unmanned space probe ever launched. It is expected to be the last "big-ticket" interplanetary explorer.

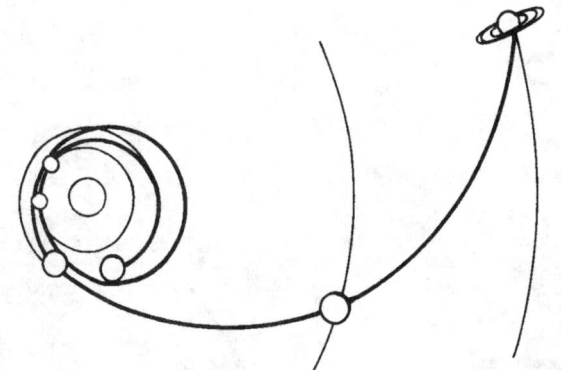

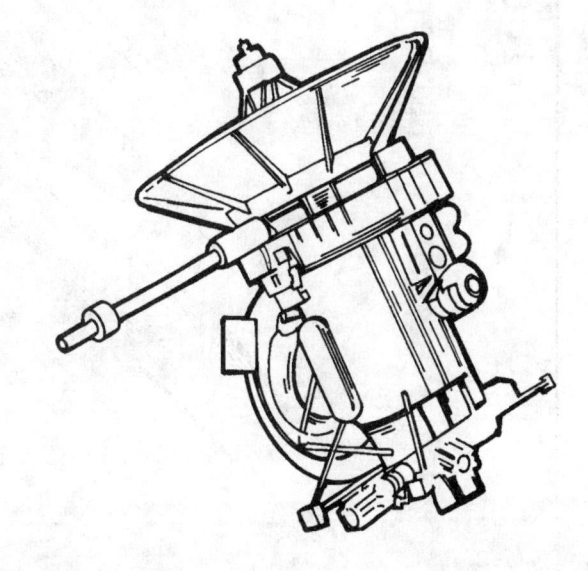

Mars—Two Views

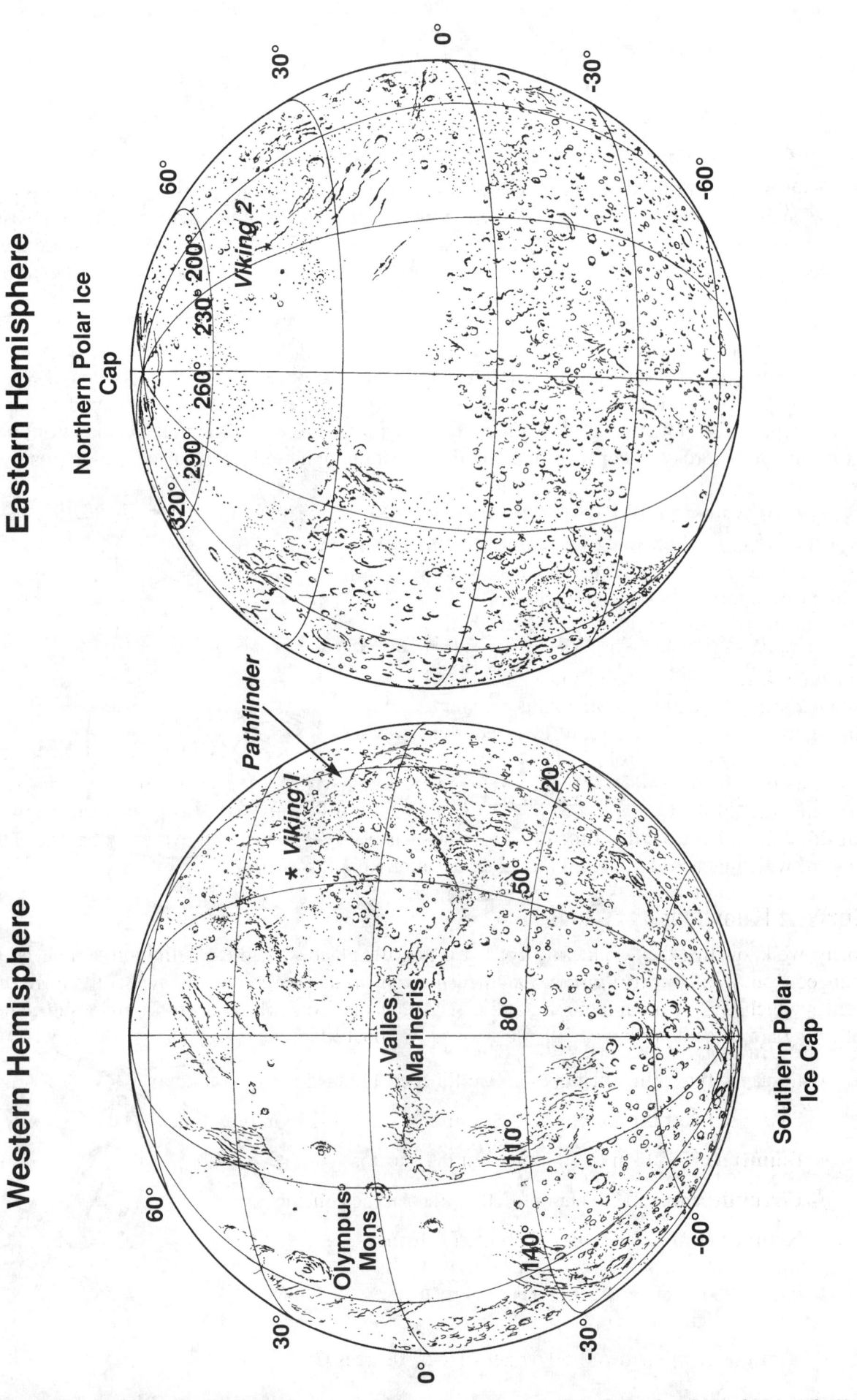

Western Hemisphere

Eastern Hemisphere

Mars

Mars History http://bang.lanl.gov/solarsys/Mars.html

The existence of this mysterious red planet has been known for centuries. Mars, like the other planets in our solar system, was recognized by early astronomers for its wandering behavior in the nighttime sky (*planetae* in Greek means *wanderer*). While stars appear to move relatively slowly in their positions night after night, planets change positions relatively quickly. This baffled early astronomers, and often planets became associated with, and even were thought to be, gods.

This planet has often been associated with fertility, farming, and war. And, even though the Romans were not the first civilization to discover Mars, they are responsible for giving it the name we are familiar with today. In fact, all the planets derive their names from Roman gods. Originally, Mars was the god of farmland and fertility. The month which marked the beginning of the Roman growing season is known as *March*, after the red planet.

Symbol of Mars

But Mars became the god of war after the Romans decided to give Mars some of the properties and characteristics of the Greek god of war, Ares. Perhaps it was Mars' red color which led to this transformation, but from that time forward, Mars has been associated with wars and battles. The word *martial*, which means *warlike*, even derives its name from this planet.

Current Knowledge of Mars

Today, we know that the "wandering gods" are actually planets. And the definition of a planet has changed from *wanderer* to a *large object which orbits the sun*. We know today that there are nine planets which revolve around the sun and that Mars is the fourth planet away from the sun. The following are some other interesting facts we know about Mars:

- **Distance from the Sun:** 206–250 million km (128–155 million miles)
- **Distance from the Earth:** 127–610 million km (79–379 million miles)
- **Diameter:** 6,760 km (4,200 miles) at the equator
- **Circumference:** 21,200 km (13,000 miles) at the equator
- **Number of Moons:** Two—Phobos and Deimos
- **Length of One Day:** 24 hours and 37 minutes (This time represents one rotation on its axis.)
- **Length of Year** (Earth days): 687 days
- **Average Temperature:** -80 degrees F (-62 degrees C)

Mars

Martian Orbit

Both Earth and Mars revolve around the sun. Earth revolves in an orbit closer to the sun than does Mars. The sun exerts a constant pull on each of the nine planets in the solar system, and those planets closest to the sun receive the greatest pull. Planets closer to the sun revolve around it in less time, and therefore a Martian year (one revolution around the sun) is longer than an Earth year. In fact, it is almost twice as long.

Mars and Earth also travel around the sun in orbits which resemble slightly elliptical circles. In fact, Mars travels in a slightly more elliptical orbit than does Earth. The illustration below shows the sun in the center of the orbits of Earth and Mars. Can you see that sometimes Earth will be closer to Mars than at other times? During these closer approaches (known as opposition), Mars will appear larger to an observer on Earth. Notice that the Earth will be close to Mars in 2001 and 2003, which are two of the years NASA has planned to launch missions to Mars. Why do you think NASA would choose to launch a mission to Mars in 2001 as opposed to 1999?

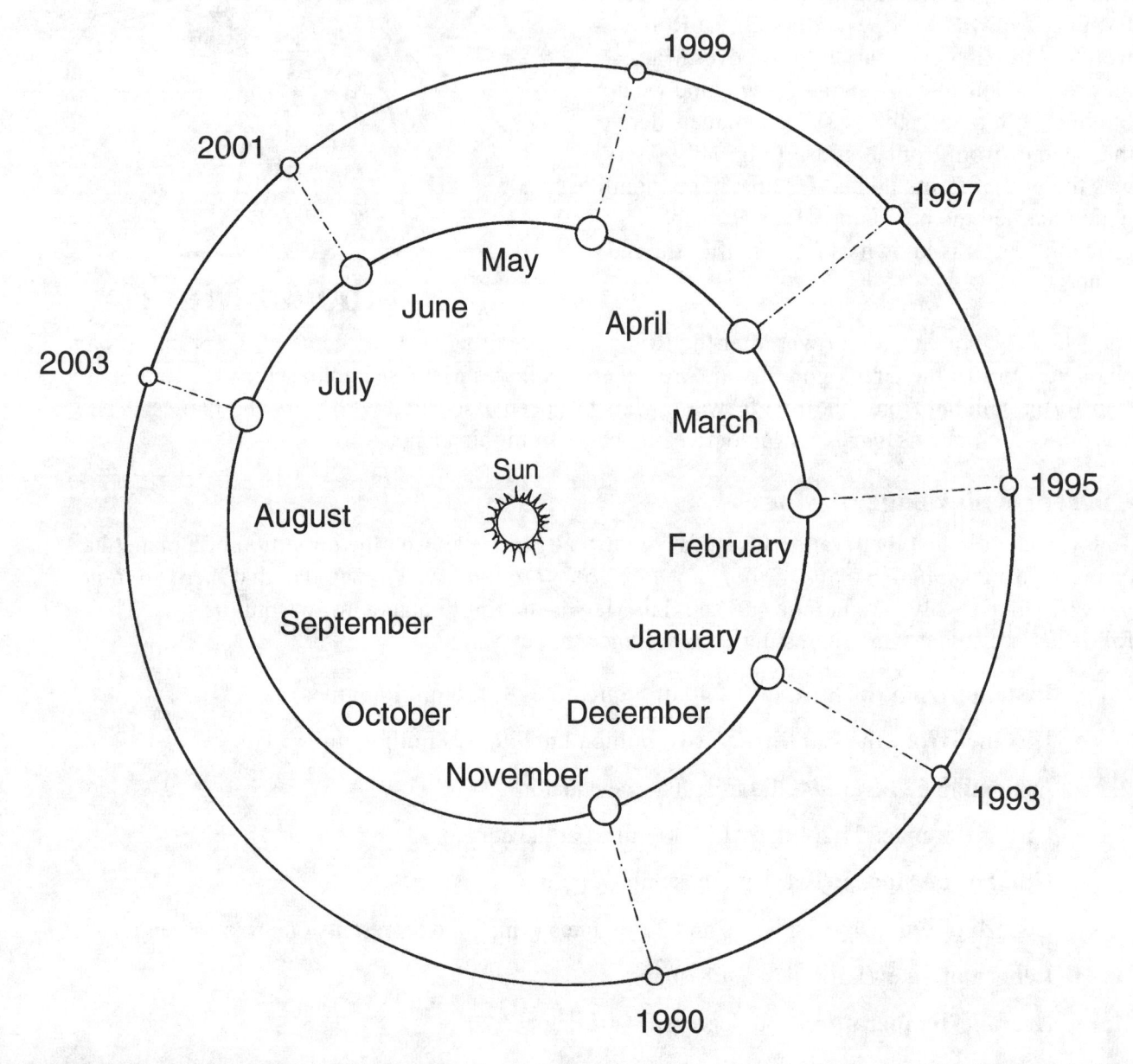

#2383 Exploring Mars and Beyond—Challenging   48   © Teacher Created Materials, Inc.

Mars

Activity #10: Martian Orbit

As Earth revolves around the sun, it is in practically the exact same position each year on the same date. For example, on January 1, 1997, Earth was in essentially the same position in its orbit around the sun as it was on January 1, 1996, 1995, 1994, etc. It is not in precisely the exact position because it takes 365 ¼ days to fully revolve around the sun one time. However, every four years we have a "leap year" which adds a day in February and puts us back on track. But for the purposes of this activity, we can assume that Earth is in the same position every year on the same date.

Look at the illustration on page 50. There are two circles made up of a series of dots. These circles represent the orbit of Earth and Mars around the sun. The inner circle is the orbit of Earth, and it is represented by 12 dots (one dot for each month of the year). The outer circle is the orbit of Mars, and it is represented by 22 dots. While Mars' year is not necessarily broken into 22 months, the 22 dots will help illustrate where Mars is located on its orbit in relation to the Earth.

How to Do the Activity

Make a photocopy of page 50 for your students. Ask the students to draw a straight line from dot #1 on the inner circle (January on Earth) to dot #1 on the outer circle. Next, they should draw a line from dot #2 on the inner circle (February on Earth) to dot #2 on the outer circle. Each numbered dot from the inner circle should have a straight line drawn to its numerical counterpart on the outer circle. The straight line represents the view the Earth has of Mars as the two planets travel around the sun. If the line passes near the sun, Mars will not be visible to Earth at that time (remember that we cannot see stars or planets when the sun is shining during the day).

When students are finished connecting the lines (there should be a total of 12 lines), they should be able to see that Earth actually passes Mars as it goes around the sun. Ask the students if a runner on a race track has an unfair advantage if she or he runs on the inside line. Have they ever noticed that the starting points on circular race tracks are offset from one another? Next time they see a track and field event on TV, ask them to pay attention to the starting points in races.

Extension

Obviously, the pattern can be continued. To do so, draw a line from #1 on the inner circle (January on Earth) to #13 on the Mars orbit. Draw a line from #2 on the inner circle (February on Earth) to #14 on the Mars orbit. Continue the pattern as long as you would like.

Mars

Activity #10: Martian Orbit (cont.)

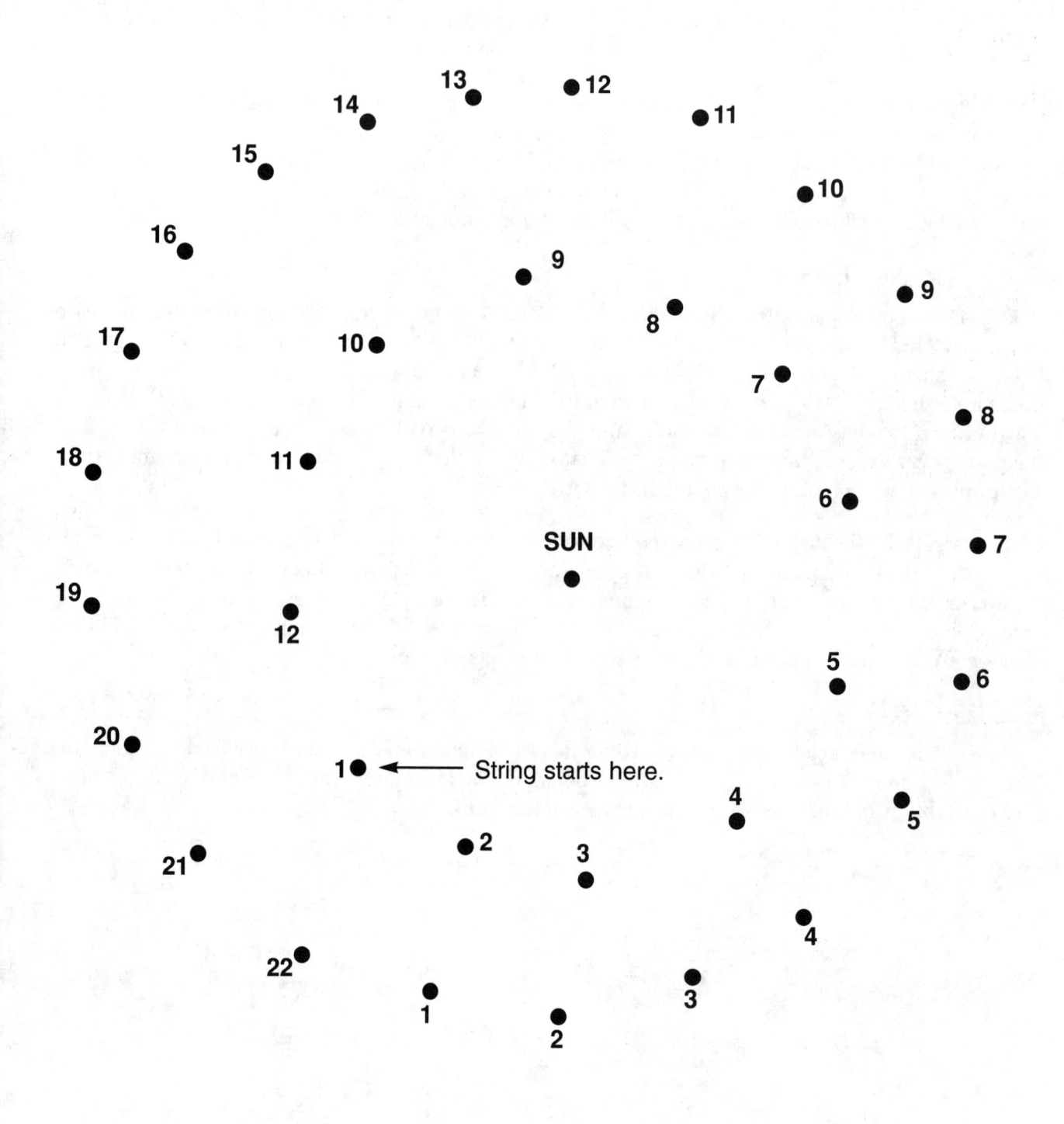

SUN

String starts here.

#2383 Exploring Mars and Beyond—Challenging   50   © Teacher Created Materials, Inc.

Activity #11: Artistic Martian Orbit

Once your students have had the opportunity to draw lines between the orbits of Earth and Mars, they may notice that the lines form a fascinating pattern. Using this pattern, a delightful art activity can be developed.

Materials

- small nails (the kind used for hanging small pictures on a wall)
- plywood
- hammer
- string
- photocopy of page 50

Procedure

1. Lay the photocopy of page 50 on top of the piece of plywood.
2. Hammer the nails into the dots in the illustration.
3. When the nails are in place, tie or wrap one end of the string around #1 on the inner circle.
4. Pull the string from #1 on the inner circle and wrap it around from the left side of #1 on the outer circle. In other words, approach the nail in position #1 on the outer circle from its left side and run the string around it on its way to the left side of #2 on the inner circle.
5. Continue by running the string around #2 on the inner circle and approach #2 on the outer circle from its left side.
6. Continue the pattern for as long as you like.
7. Remove the paper template when finished.

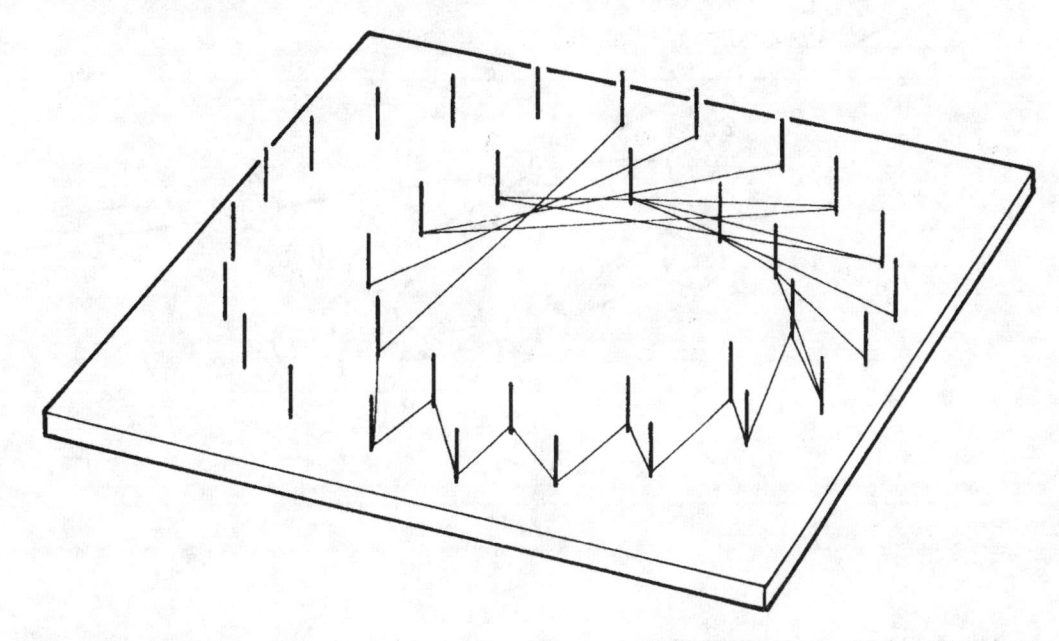

Mars

Retrograde Motion

When you drive along the freeway, you will often pass a car which will sometimes pass you at a later time. In other words, that car may at times be ahead of you and at other times be behind you. If you recall the activity on page 50 where you drew a line between the positions of Earth and Mars as they traveled around the sun, you could see how they continue to play a game of pass-and-catch-up as they go around. Just like the cars on the freeway, Earth and Mars continue to swap positions.

Ancient astronomers had a hard time trying to figure out why a planet like Mars would appear to be moving in one direction for a series of evenings and then appear to be moving in the opposite direction for another series of evenings. Of course, ancient astronomers did not have the benefit of knowing what we know now about the orbits of the planets. They didn't realize that Earth was riding on an inside track! In fact, they thought that everything in the universe revolved around the planet Earth.

This forward and backward motion of the planets in the nighttime sky is called *retrograde motion*, and it is one of the pieces of evidence which led forward-thinking astronomers such as Copernicus to doubt that the Earth was the center of the universe. Copernicus' heliocentric (sun-centered) theory of the universe would account for this strange motion of the planets.

Below is an illustration of the position of Mars in the nighttime sky as it appears here on Earth over a six-month period in which Mars is approached and then passed by Earth. On page 53, there is an illustration which shows why this retrograde motion is occurring. You can make an overhead transparency of page 53 and show it to your students.

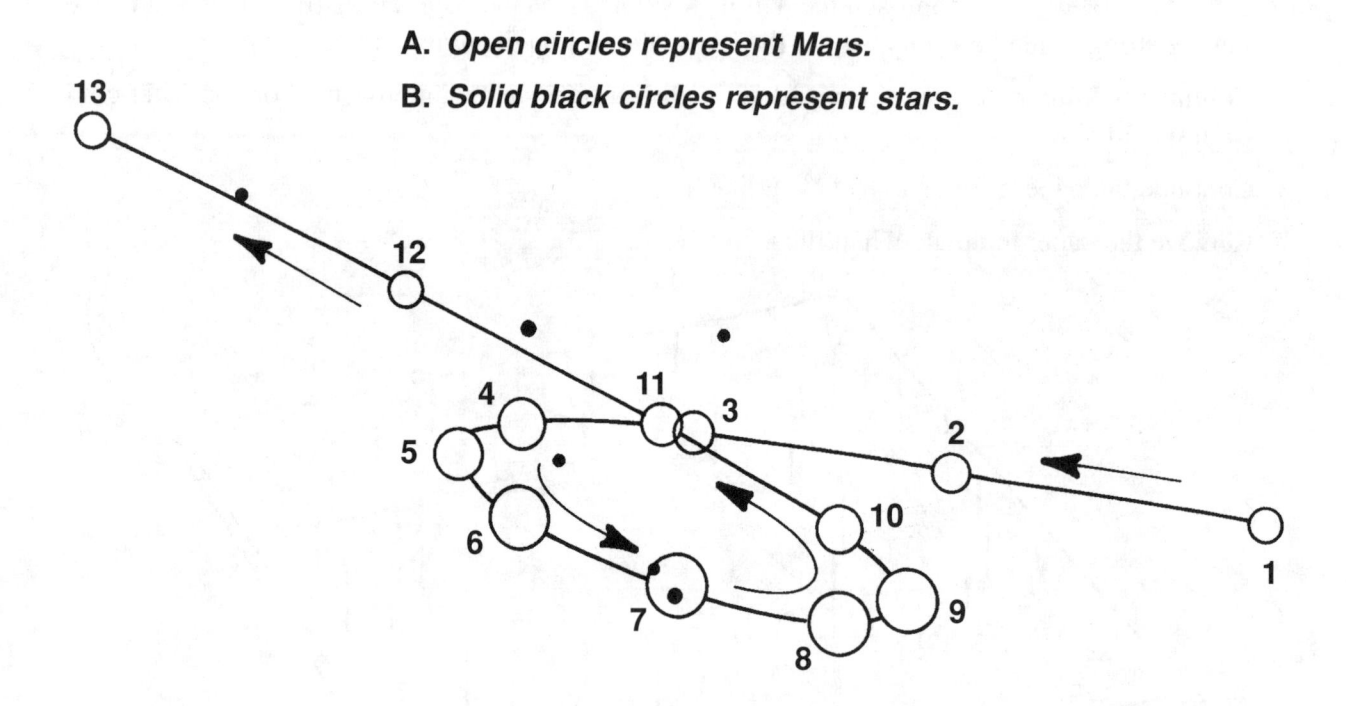

A. *Open circles represent Mars.*
B. *Solid black circles represent stars.*

#2383 *Exploring Mars and Beyond—Challenging*

Retrograde Motion *(cont.)*

Mars' Apparent Path in the Sky

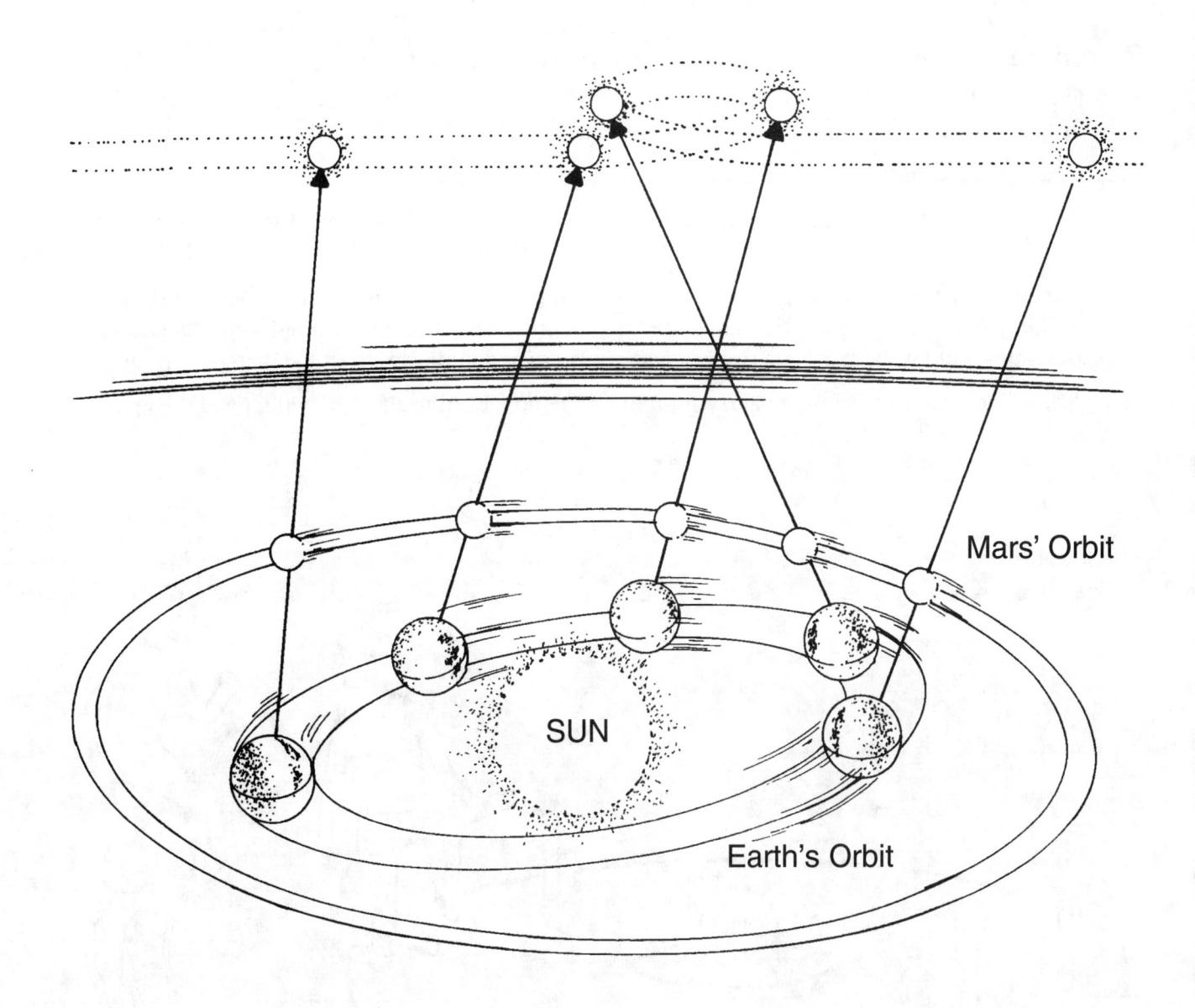

Mars' Orbit

SUN

Earth's Orbit

Activity #12: Retrograde Motion

In order for students to understand retrograde motion and the changing distance between Earth and Mars, the following activity is suggested.

Materials

- merry-go-round
- tennis ball

Procedure

1. Draw an ellipse around the merry-go-round. This ellipse can be drawn with a stick in the dirt or by using markers (such as small rocks) to outline the ellipse.
2. One student should stand on the outer edge of the merry-go-round.
3. Another student should stand at one point on the ellipse. They should stand so they face each other.
4. Start the merry-go-round at a slow speed and ask the student standing on the ground to start walking along the ellipse in the same direction the merry-go-round is turning. The student who is walking should walk at a normal speed and not try to match the speed of the merry-go-round.
5. Ask the student who is on the merry-go-round if he notices himself approaching and then passing the student on the ground.

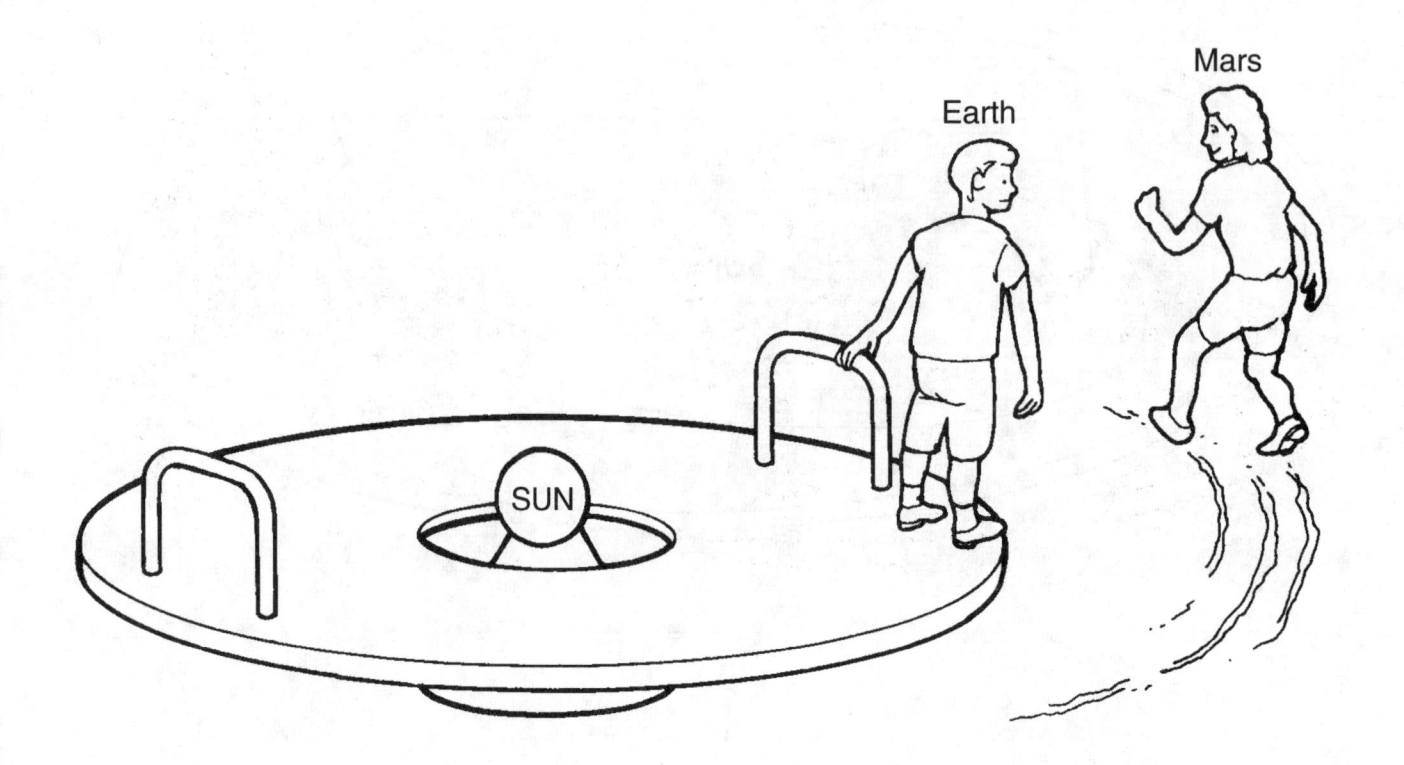

Mars

Activity #12: Retrograde Motion *(cont.)*

This demonstration raises a number of interesting issues about the Earth and Mars' orbital relationship. Read the following discussion topics and discuss these with your students as they carry out the merry-go-round activity.

1. **Who's Who**

    Obviously, the student on the merry-go-round is the Earth, and the student on the ground is Mars. The sun is in the center of the merry-go-round.

2. **How to Hit a Moving Target**

    See if a stationary student on the ground can successfully toss a tennis ball to the student on the merry-go-round at a pre-determined spot on his or her orbit around the sun. The students will notice that for a successful "launch," the tennis ball will need to be released before the student on the merry-go-round reaches the pre-determined spot.* Look on page 66 at the illustration of the *Pathfinder* spacecraft's route to Mars. Notice that it too is released before Earth and Mars reach their closest position. It takes time for a spacecraft to travel from Earth to Mars, and therefore the rocket is not aimed at where Mars *is* on the launch day but rather where it ***will be*** on the day the spacecraft arrives.

    * While it appears you will be launching a probe from Mars to Earth in this demonstration, it illustrates the point that to hit a moving target, one must anticipate its future location. This demonstration may not be as visually effective if you have an Earth-to-Mars launch.

Activity #12: Retrograde Motion *(cont.)*

3. **Do Planets Come Out Only at Night?**

   Sunlight prevents us from seeing any stars or planets during the day. When it is daytime, the stars and planets are still up in the sky but are not visible because the sun is so much brighter. On the merry-go-round model, however, we must imagine the sun to be in the center and, therefore, the two student planets will be able to see each other constantly. To truly be able to see what people on Earth see, the student who is riding on the merry-go-round should always be looking straight away from the merry-go-round (into space) and not across the center of the merry-go-round (the sun).

4. **Here It Comes . . . There It Goes**

   Ask the students who ride on the merry-go-round (Earth) to take careful notice of their head movements as they keep an eye on the student on the ground (Mars). Do they notice that as they approach the student their heads are turned one way, and as they pass the student their heads are turned the other way? This is an illustration of retrograde motion. Mars appears to be coming at Earth from one direction, only to suddenly change direction when it is passed.

   To an observer on Earth, this phenomenon looks as if Mars has changed direction. And up until the Copernican heliocentric model of the solar system was accepted, earthbound astronomers assumed that Mars was changing direction.

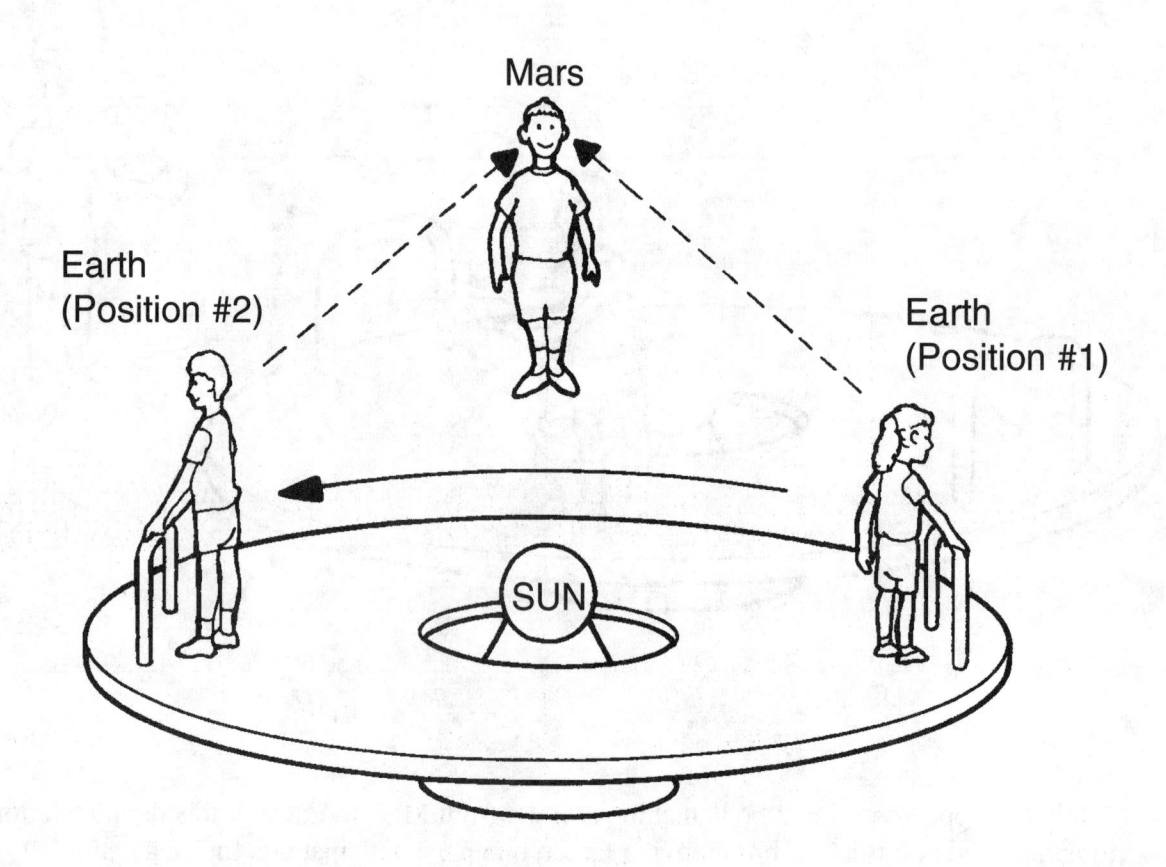

Unmanned Missions to Mars

Chronology

The following is a table which displays the chronology of missions to Mars. For more extensive information, you can visit the National Space Science Data Center's (NSSDC) Web site at **http://nssdc.gsfc.nasa.gov/planetary** and click on the Chronology of Lunar and Planetary Exploration. At that same site, you can find information about each one of these missions to Mars if you click on Information by Project.

Mission	Type	Nation	Dates*
Mariner 4	Flyby	U.S.	1965
Mariner 6	Flyby	U.S.	1969
Mariner 7	Flyby	U.S.	1969
Mars 2	Orbiter	USSR	1971
Mars 2	Lander	USSR	1971
Mars 3	Orbiter	USSR	1971
Mars 3	Lander	USSR	1971
Mariner 9	Orbiter	U.S.	1971–72
Mars 4	Orbiter	USSR	1974
Mars 5	Orbiter	USSR	1974
Mars 6	Lander	USSR	1974
Viking 1	Orbiter	U.S.	1976–80
Viking 1	Lander	U.S.	1976–82
Viking 2	Orbiter	U.S.	1976–78
Viking 2	Lander	U.S.	1976–80
Phobos	Orbiter	USSR	1988–89
Mars *Observer*	Orbiter	U.S.	1993 (failed)
Mars '96	Orbiter/Lander	USSR	1996 (failed)

* Dates include the year the spacecraft reached Mars and was in operation at Mars.

Unmanned Missions to Mars

USSR/Russia Missions

Mars (USSR) http://nssdc.gsfc.nasa.gov/planetary

Between 1971 and 1974, the Soviet Union launched five unmanned spacecraft to Mars. *Mars 2–6* were designed as a series of missions to either fly by the planet, drop into its orbit, or land on its surface. Officially, the Soviet Union was the first country to land an object on Mars with *Mars 2* when it crash-landed on November 27, 1971. Sadly, the probe was destroyed during the landing and was not able to return any data. Not until *Viking* landed in 1976 would there be data or pictures returned from the surface of Mars.

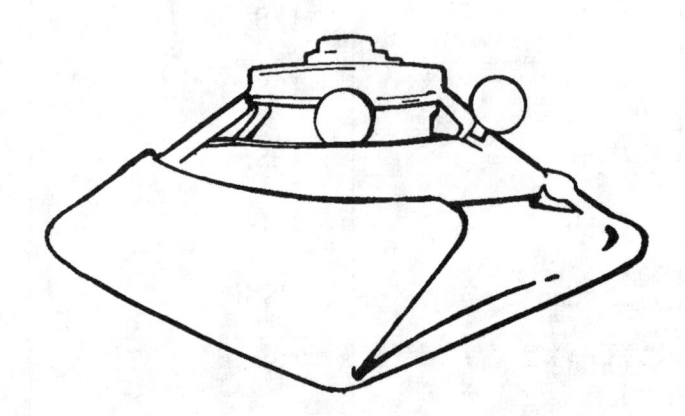

Mars '96 (Russia) http://nssdc.gsfc.nasa.gov/planetary

Originally named *Mars '94* with an intended launch date in 1994, this Russian mission to Mars ended in tragedy on the night of its launch. Launched on November 16, 1996, *Mars '96's* fourth stage failed to fire properly, and the spacecraft crashed back to Earth near the coast of Chile. With the crash of *Mars '96*, the future of Russian planetary exploration has been cast into doubt.

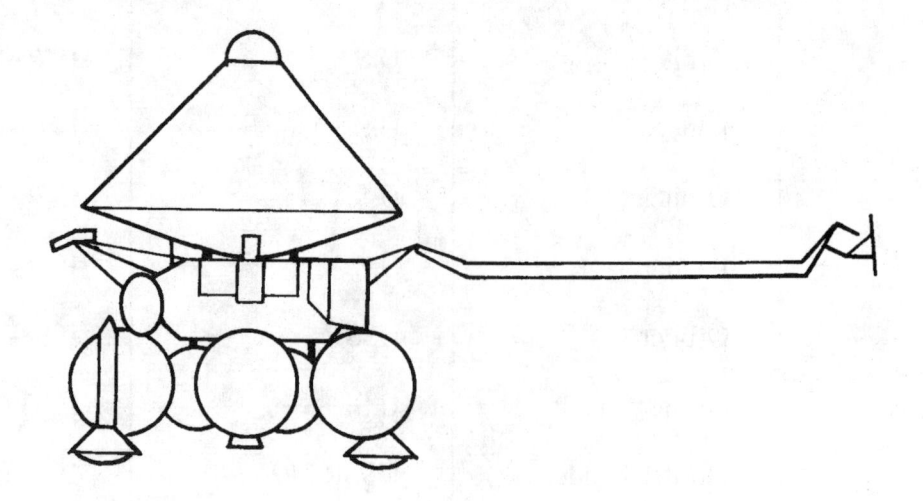

#2383 Exploring Mars and Beyond—Challenging   58   © Teacher Created Materials, Inc.

Unmanned Missions to Mars

Mariner

Mariner http://nssdc.gsfc.nasa.gov/planetary

Mariner 4 was the very first successful mission to Mars. It was launched in 1964 and flew by Mars on July 14, 1965. It got as close as 9,844 km (6113 mi) and took 22 pictures. *Mariner 4* found Mars to be a desolate planet with no signs of life, but it found frost in the crater rims.

Following *Mariner 4*'s successful flyby of Mars, the United States and the USSR turned their attention toward the manned moon landing (which happened on July 20, 1969) and left Mars alone for a while. These *Mariners* found evidence of volcanoes and a heavily cratered southern hemisphere. *Mariner 9*, in 1971, holds the honor of being the first spacecraft to ever successfully orbit around planet Mars. *Mariner 9* mapped 85% of the planet's surface, took the first pictures of Mars' two moons, Phobos and Deimos, and discovered a large rift valley along the equator of the planet. This rift valley was later named *Valles Mariner* after the *Mariner* spacecraft.

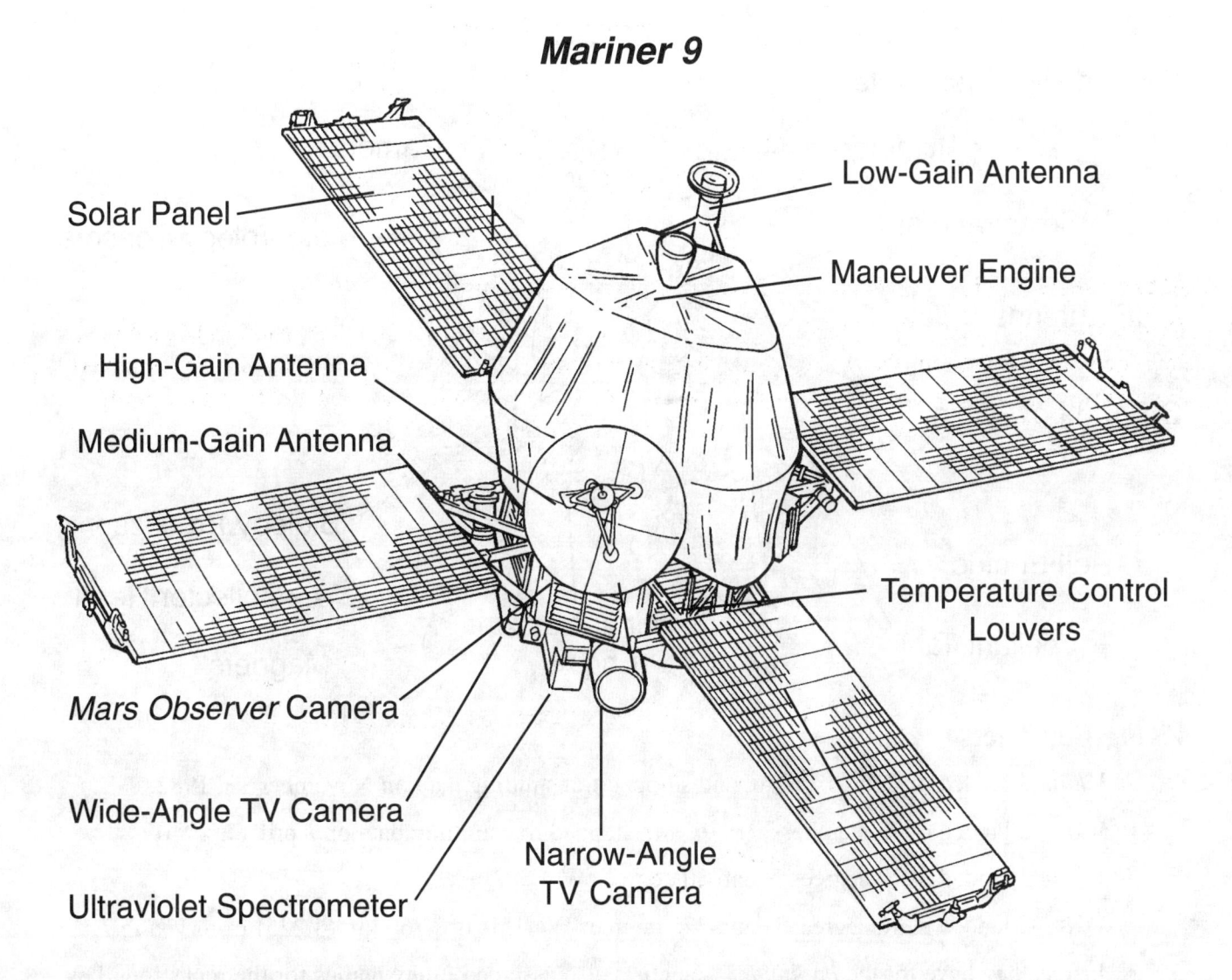

Mariner 9

Labeled parts:
- Solar Panel
- Low-Gain Antenna
- Maneuver Engine
- High-Gain Antenna
- Medium-Gain Antenna
- Temperature Control Louvers
- *Mars Observer* Camera
- Wide-Angle TV Camera
- Narrow-Angle TV Camera
- Ultraviolet Spectrometer

Unmanned Missions to Mars

Viking

Viking http://nssdc.gsfc.nasa.gov/planetary

By the time the *Viking* landers were launched in 1975, the USSR had already made several unsuccessful attempts at landing a craft on the Martian surface. Now it was the United States' turn to attempt a landing. *Viking 1* was launched on August 20, 1975, and was followed by *Viking 2* on September 9, 1975. The idea was to launch two landers in the hopes that at least one would work. As it turned out, both were very successful.

The *Viking* landers had a variety of mission objectives. One was to identify the elements and minerals present in the soil, another was to record any seismic activity (e.g., Earthquakes—or "Marsquakes") and one was to look for life. In particular, the *Viking* landers were looking for signs of photosynthesis when they were looking for life. They would scoop up some soil and place it in an on-board machine which would simulate the conditions needed for life. *Viking* found no signs of life. The illustration below shows what the *Viking* landers looked like.

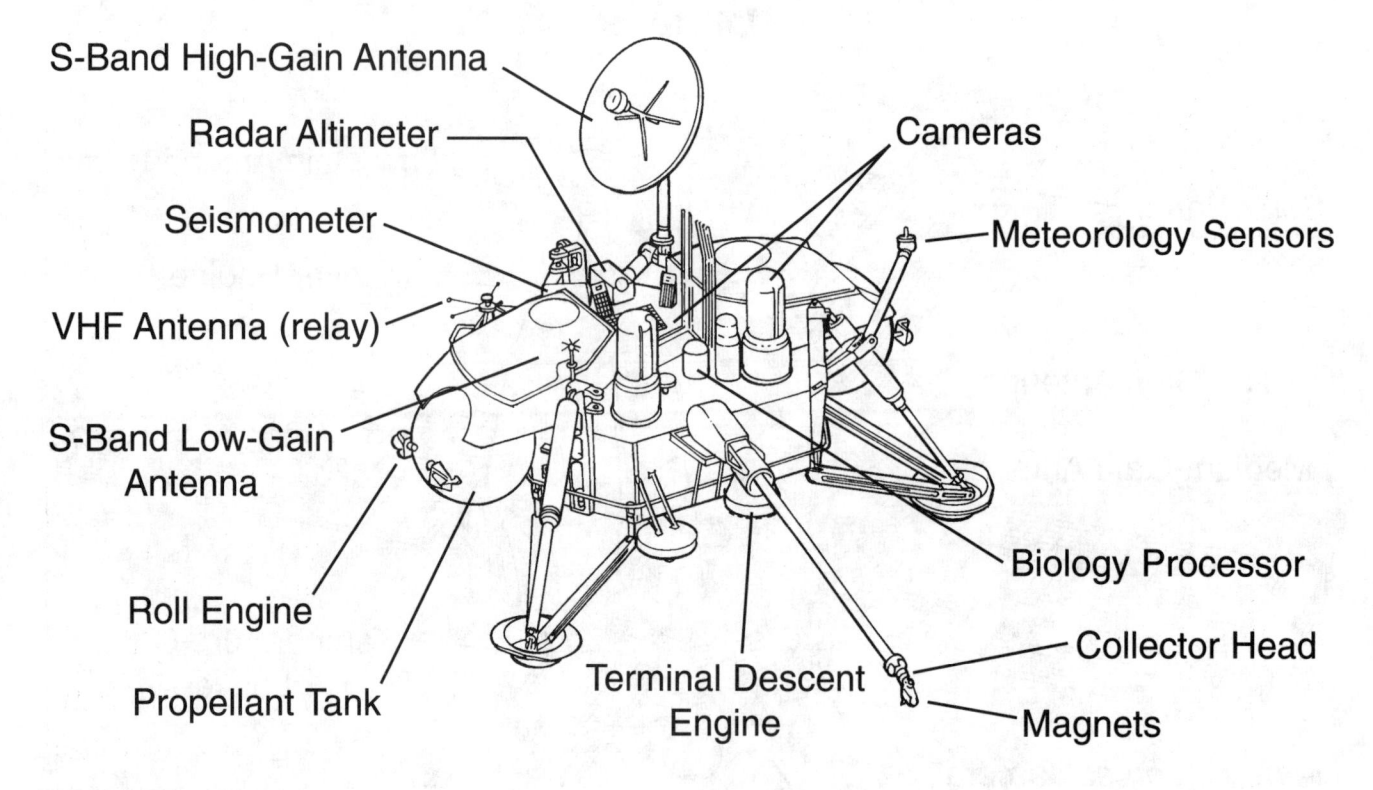

Viking Fun Facts

- *Viking 1* landed on July 20, 1976, and stopped transmitting data on November 13, 1982.
- *Viking 2* landed on September 3, 1976, and stopped transmitting data on April 11, 1980.
- *Viking 1* landed at 22 degrees N and 50 degrees W.
- *Viking 2* landed at 46 degrees N and 225 degrees W. This is 6,760 km (4,225) from *Viking 1*.
- Just as they have for the *Pathfinder*, scientists also assigned funny names for the rocks found by *Viking*. Two of those names were "Midas Muffler" and "Big Joe."

Unmanned Missions to Mars

Mars *Observer*

Mars *Observer* http://nssdc.gsfc.nasa.gov/planetary

Launched on September 25, 1992, atop a Titan 3 booster rocket, the $1 billion Mars *Observer* was supposed to mark America's return to Mars after the *Viking* missions of the 1970s. The *Observer* was supposed to go into a polar orbit around Mars and map its surface. This mapping would have provided scientists with the information they would need to determine landing sites for future unmanned and manned missions. Further, the *Observer* was to serve as a communications relay for the upcoming Russian probe, *Mars '94* (see page 58), which was to land on the surface of Mars. Unfortunately, the *Observer* lost radio contact with NASA's Jet Propulsion Laboratory (JPL) on August 21, 1993, and has not been heard from since. To this day, no one knows what happened to *Observer*.

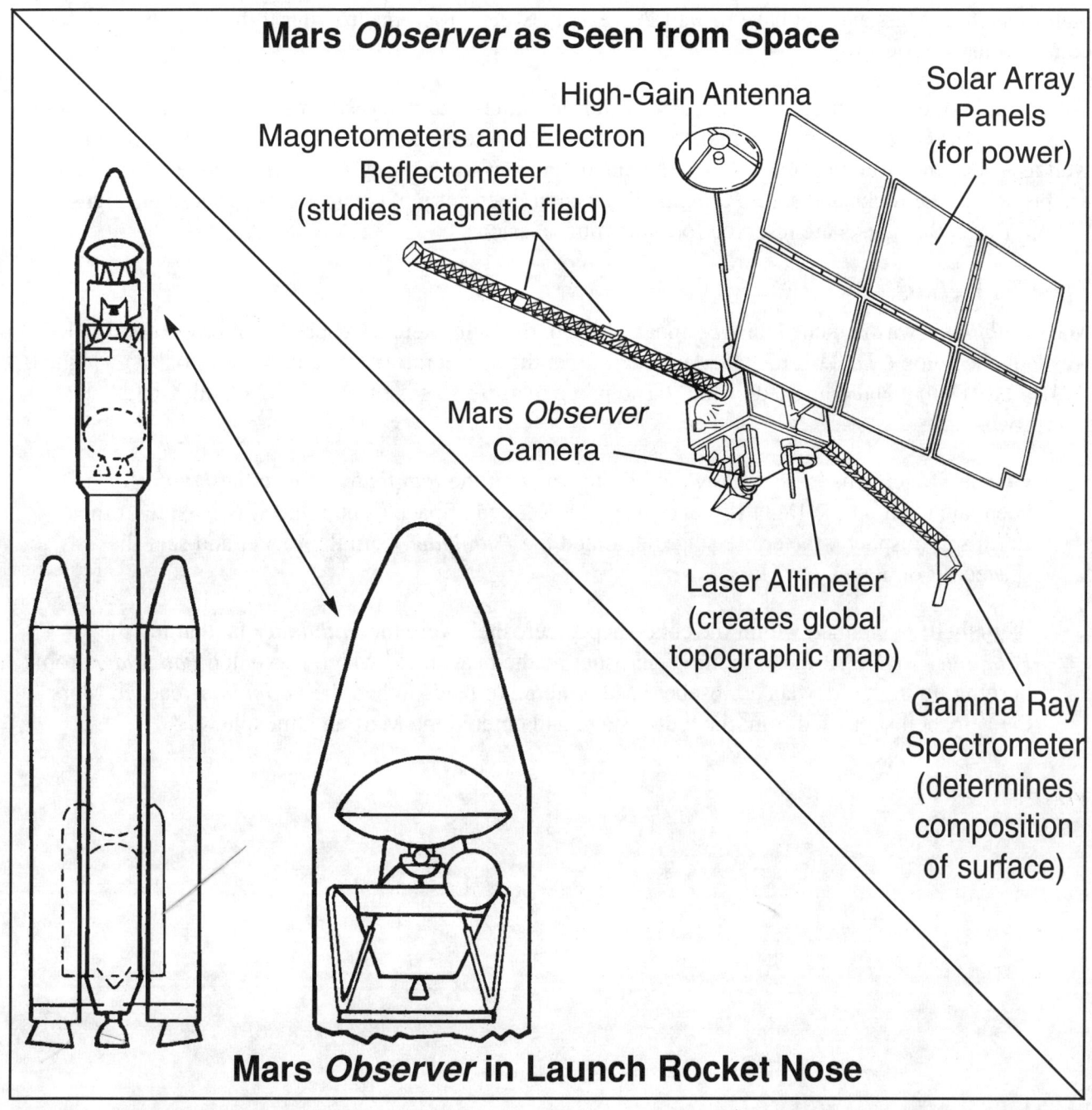

Mars *Observer* as Seen from Space

- High-Gain Antenna
- Magnetometers and Electron Reflectometer (studies magnetic field)
- Solar Array Panels (for power)
- Mars *Observer* Camera
- Laser Altimeter (creates global topographic map)
- Gamma Ray Spectrometer (determines composition of surface)

Mars *Observer* in Launch Rocket Nose

Unmanned Missions to Mars

Mars *Pathfinder*

Mars *Pathfinder* http://mpfwww.jpl.nasa.gov

It has been a little over 20 years since NASA has put a spacecraft on the surface of Mars. The last time was in 1976 when two landers named *Viking 1* and *Viking 2* (see page 60) touched down on Martian soil. *Pathfinder* marks the first of a series of returns to the red planet scheduled to occur over the next several years.

At a cost of $250 million and after four years of development, the Mars *Pathfinder* mission is one of a series of new space probes designed to be faster, smaller, and cheaper than previous planetary missions. NASA's new goal is to design and develop a series of missions to Mars which will have specific objectives for each mission. In this way, NASA hopes to be able to launch more frequent missions to planets such as Mars and not have to wait 20 years between programs in order to build a very comprehensive spacecraft.

For example, the mission objectives of *Pathfinder* are quite clear and distinct from the other upcoming missions. *Pathfinder's* mission is to determine how well a rover can work on the surface of Mars as well as to test the structure of Martian atmosphere and surface geology and to determine what elements are present in the rocks and soil. *Pathfinder's* mission does not include any tests for possible signs of life on Mars. Such tests are reserved for upcoming missions.

Specific Details

Mars *Pathfinder* was launched on December 4, 1996, from the Kennedy Space Center in Florida. It was launched atop a Delta II rocket. At launch time, the spacecraft (not including the rocket) weighed 870 kg (1,914 lbs) and consisted of four basic parts: a cruise stage, an aeroshell, a lander, and a microrover.

>   **Cruise Stage:** This is essentially the driving force of the *Pathfinder*. Once the *Pathfinder* had been launched on the Delta II rocket from the Kennedy Space Center and was outside of the Earth's atmosphere, the cruise stage separated the *Pathfinder* from the rocket and sent the spacecraft on its way to Mars.
>
>   **Aeroshell:** Contained within the cone-shaped aeroshell were the *Pathfinder* lander and the *Pathfinder* rover. At the base of the aeroshell is the heat shield which prevented *Pathfinder* from burning up in the Martian atmosphere as it entered to land. When the *Pathfinder* reached Mars, the aeroshell separated from the cruise stage and entered the Martian atmosphere.

Unmanned Missions to Mars

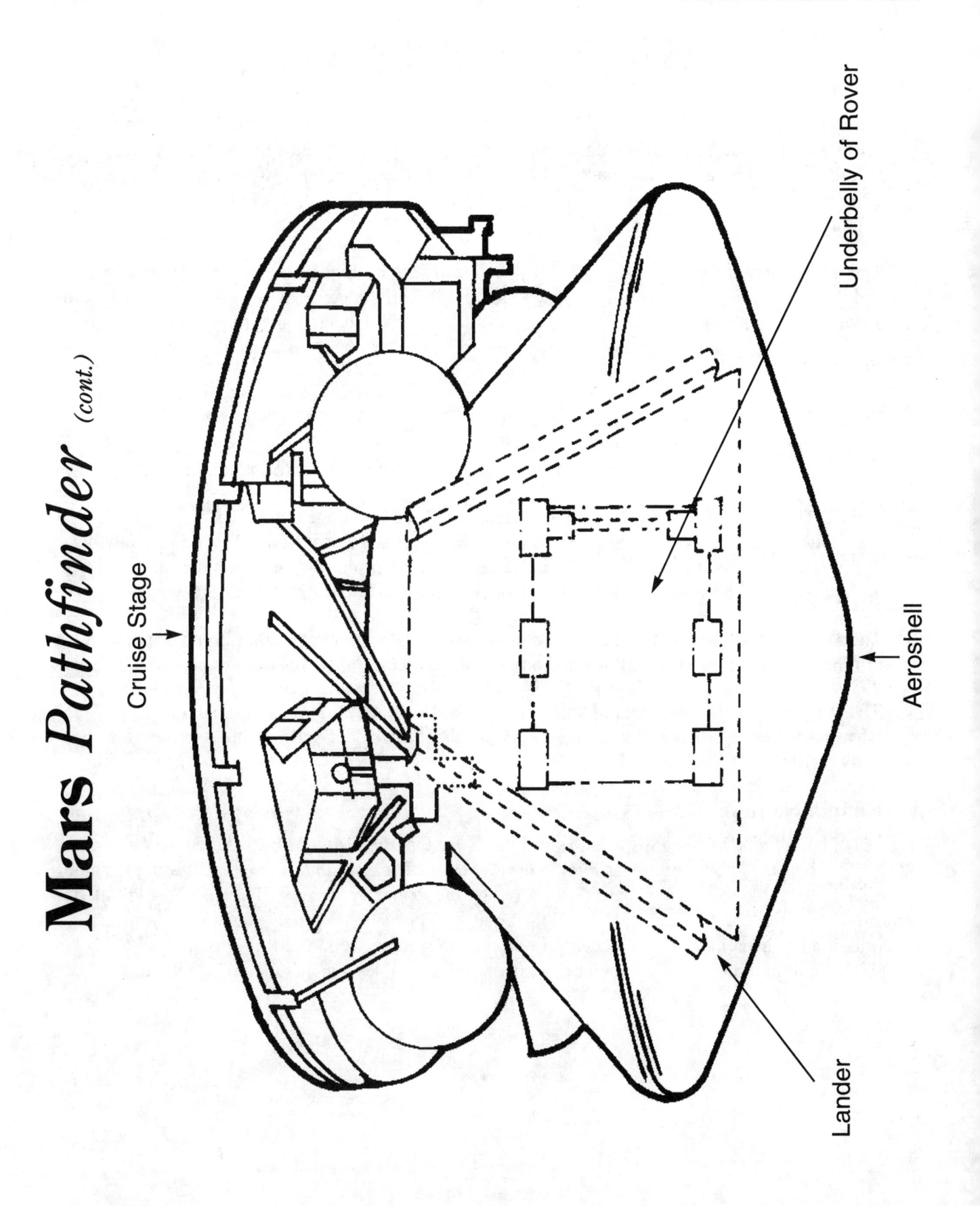

Mars *Pathfinder* (cont.)

Cruise Stage

Underbelly of Rover

Aeroshell

Lander

© Teacher Created Materials, Inc. 63 #2383 *Exploring Mars and Beyond—Challenging*

Mars *Pathfinder* (cont.)

Lander: The lander emerged from the aeroshell once the heat of entering the Martian atmosphere subsided and it had been slowed down considerably by a parachute attached to the aeroshell. Finally, the lander came to rest on the Martian surface after bouncing to a landing on a series of air bags (much like those found in cars). (For more information on the details of the actual landing, look on pages 65 and 66.)

This illustration of the lander shows it fully deployed with each of its three solar panels laid out and the rover sitting on one of those panels. During flight, the lander is folded up like the bud of a flower before it opens its petals. While it is folded up, the lander is able to protect the precious cargo it carries by holding everything close together in order for it to survive the stress of space flight.

The lander itself has a mass of 325 kg (715 lbs) and contains its own camera (which is responsible, among other things, for taking pictures of the rover as it moves about the Martian surface), weather devices, and a communication device for relaying information to Earth.

Rover: The *Pathfinder's* rover is a six-wheeled, 16-kg (35 lbs) dune buggy designed to roll over the surface of Mars to collect information about the rocks and soil it finds. It is powered by the 0.2 square meter solar panel located on its surface, and it has an on-board computer powered by an Intel 80C85 8-bit processor which can process some 100,000 instructions per second.

The rover, also known as *Sojourner*, is 28 cm high (11 inches), 63 cm long (25 inches) and 48 cm (19 inches) wide. Its wheels allow the body to ride 13 cm (5 inches) above the ground.

The *Pathfinder* lander landed right on time—July 4, 1997, at 12:57 P.M. EDT. And just two days later, the *Sojourner* rover rolled off one of the petals of the lander and onto the surface of Mars (July 6, 1997, at 1:40 A.M. EDT).

What's in a Name?

Originally, the *Pathfinder* mission was known as the *Mars Environmental Survey* (MESUR) *Pathfinder*, and finally it became known simply as *Pathfinder* (Whew!). The *Pathfinder* rover was given the name *Sojourner* following a worldwide contest sponsored by the Planetary Society. Twelve-year-old Valerie Ambrose from Bridgeport, Connecticut, won the contest. This is not the first time nor the last time a space mission has been named by a student. Look in the resource section of this book to find out how to get information on the Planetary Society and perhaps be eligible to name upcoming missions.

Unmanned Missions to Mars

Mars *Pathfinder* (cont.)

The Mars *Pathfinder* and its rover, *Sojourner*, have three main instruments on board to help carry out their mission. These instruments are as follows:

Imager for Mars *Pathfinder* (IMP)

The pictures you have seen of the surface of Mars and those of the *Sojourner* rover itself are all taken by this IMP camera which is located on the *Pathfinder* lander. This camera is specially equipped to take stereoscopic images of the surface of Mars. In other words, it can take 3-D pictures. There are also smaller cameras located on the *Sojourner* rover. You can find out more about the IMP and even print out some 3-D images from its Web site: **http://ww.lpl.arizona.edu/imp**

Atmospheric Structure Instrument/Meteorology Experiment (ASI/MET)

Temperature and weather conditions will affect the *Pathfinder* mission as well as any future missions to the surface of the planet. This device, located on the lander, is designed to collect data on temperature and weather on Mars. In fact, if you want to know what the weather is like on Mars today, you can check out the following Web site: **http://mpfwww.jpl.nasa.gov/ops/asimet.html**

Alpha-Proton X-Ray Spectrometer (APXS)

This is the main instrument on the *Sojourner* rover. The APXS contains a supply of radioactive Curium-244 which will emit x-rays so that the rover can analyze what chemical elements are present in the Martian soil. The reddish color of the soil is caused by the same element (iron) that causes reddish soil here on Earth. But scientists have been excited to learn that quartz (a mineral composed of the elements silicon and oxygen) was found in a rock they called *Barnacle Bill*. The presence of quartz suggests volcanic and plate tectonic activity on Mars.

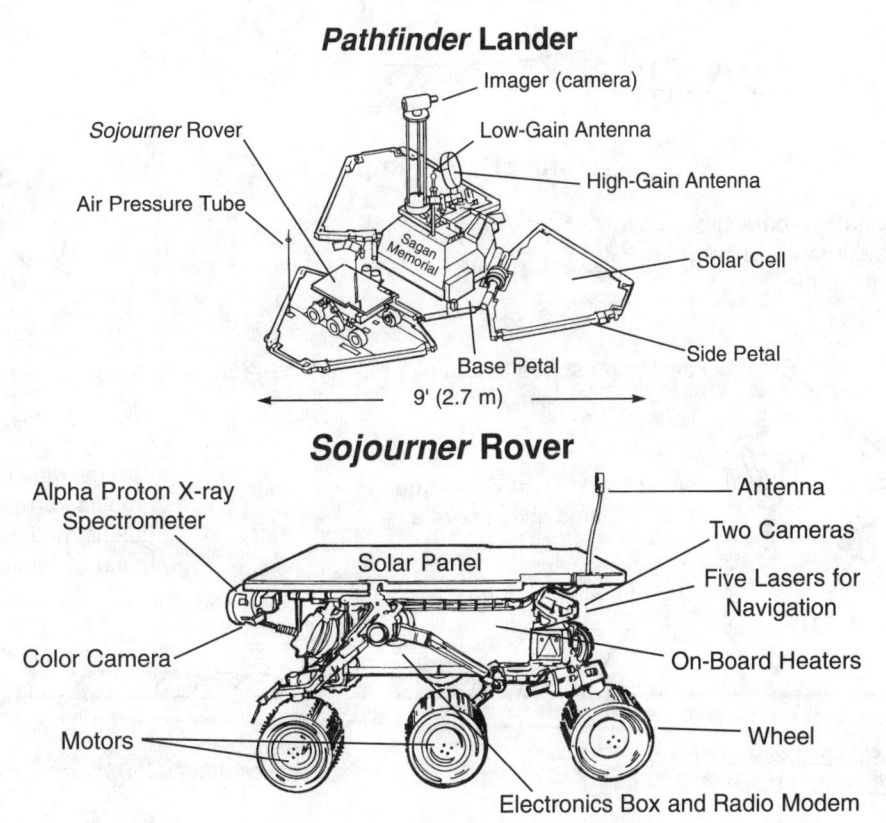

***Pathfinder* Lander**

Sojourner Rover · Imager (camera) · Low-Gain Antenna · High-Gain Antenna · Air Pressure Tube · Solar Cell · Base Petal · Side Petal · 9' (2.7 m)

***Sojourner* Rover**

Alpha Proton X-ray Spectrometer · Antenna · Two Cameras · Solar Panel · Five Lasers for Navigation · Color Camera · On-Board Heaters · Motors · Wheel · Electronics Box and Radio Modem

© Teacher Created Materials, Inc.

Unmanned Missions to Mars

Pathfinder's Journey

At this point, your students should have developed some background into the history and future of Mars exploration (e.g., *Mariner, Viking,* and missions by the Soviet Union) as well as some understanding of some of the basic astronomical principles involved in planetary astronomy (e.g., retrograde motion and the relative positions of Mars and Earth during their orbits).

Now it is time to examine the flight plan of the Mars *Pathfinder* mission! Below is an illustration of the path taken by *Pathfinder* to Mars as well as an illustration and a description of *Pathfinder's* entry, descent, and landing on Mars.

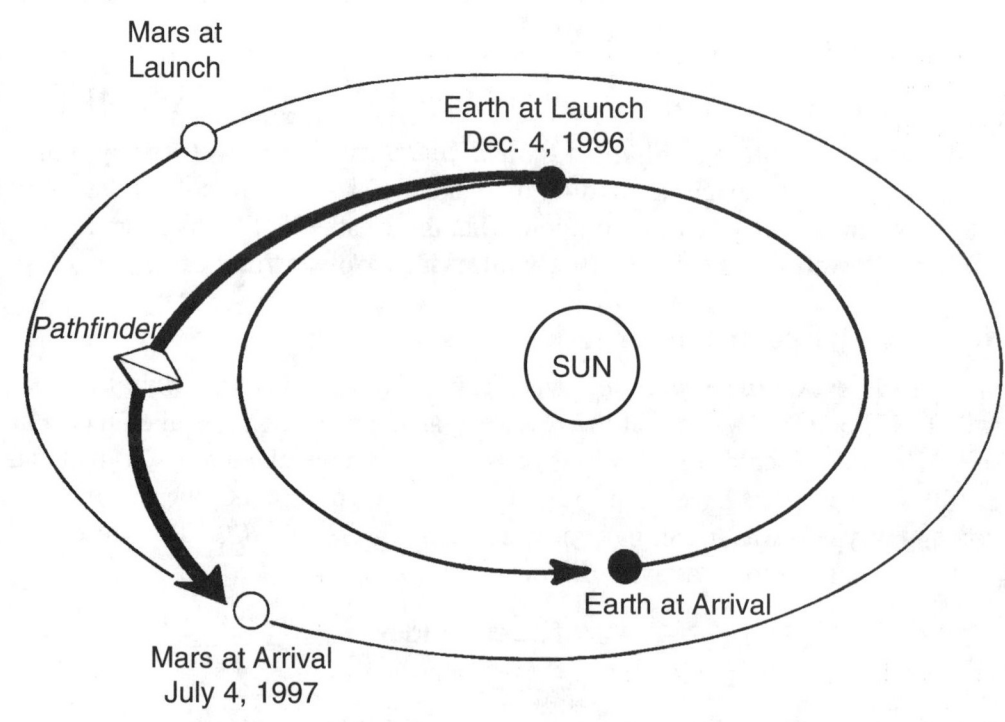

Mars at Launch

Earth at Launch
Dec. 4, 1996

Pathfinder

SUN

Earth at Arrival

Mars at Arrival
July 4, 1997

Just Before Impact

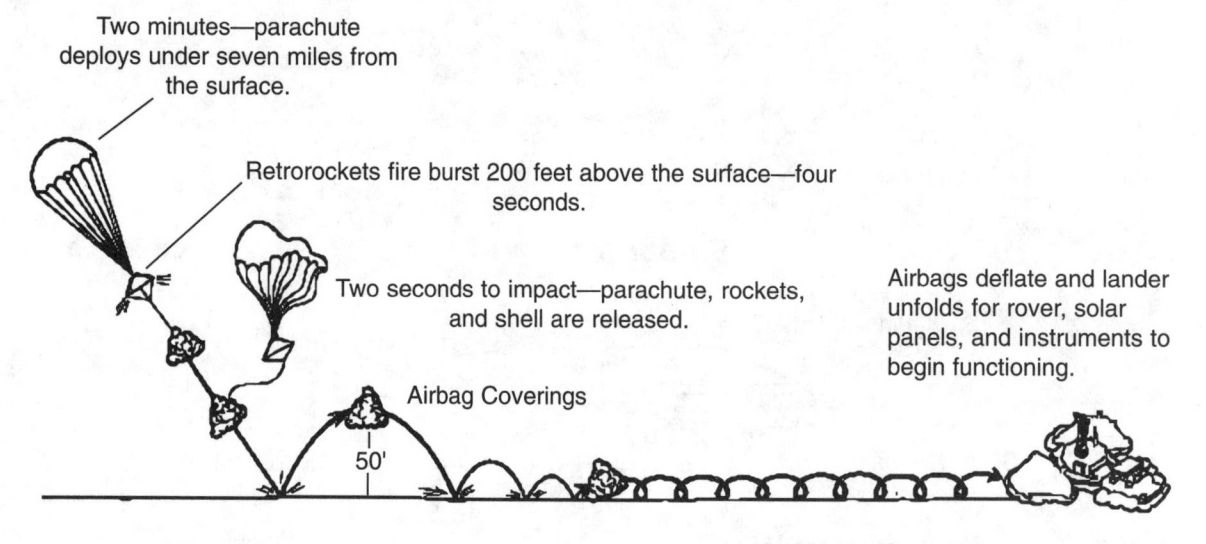

Two minutes—parachute deploys under seven miles from the surface.

Retrorockets fire burst 200 feet above the surface—four seconds.

Two seconds to impact—parachute, rockets, and shell are released.

Airbags deflate and lander unfolds for rover, solar panels, and instruments to begin functioning.

Airbag Coverings

50'

Strikes Mars at 22 mph. (35 kph)

Roll continues for 92 seconds.

Unmanned Missions to Mars

Activity #13: Hitting a Moving Target

Realize that it took some time for the *Pathfinder* spacecraft to reach Mars. After it was launched from Earth, *Pathfinder* traveled a little over 575 days to get to Mars. While it was moving through space at an incredible 26,700 km/hr (16,600 mph), it still had to cover a trajectory of 500 million km (310 million miles)! This becomes extremely complicated when you realize that neither Mars nor Earth will be standing still as *Pathfinder* moves toward its final destination.

Basically, the scientists at JPL had to aim *Pathfinder* so it would run into Mars at a location it wasn't in on December 4, 1996 (*Pathfinder's* launch date). This required knowledge of Mars' orbital speed around the sun. A good illustration of this trajectory is available on page 66.

In order to give your students an understanding of how difficult it is to hit a moving target, the following activity is recommended:

Materials

- tennis ball
- toy race car (e.g., Hot Wheels)
- ramp
- footstool

Procedure

1. Ask one student to stand on the footstool at a safe height and hold the tennis ball.
2. Ask another student to roll the race car down the ramp toward the student on the footstool.
3. The student on the footstool should be instructed to drop the ball straight down. She is to drop the ball so that it will strike the car as it passes underneath her.

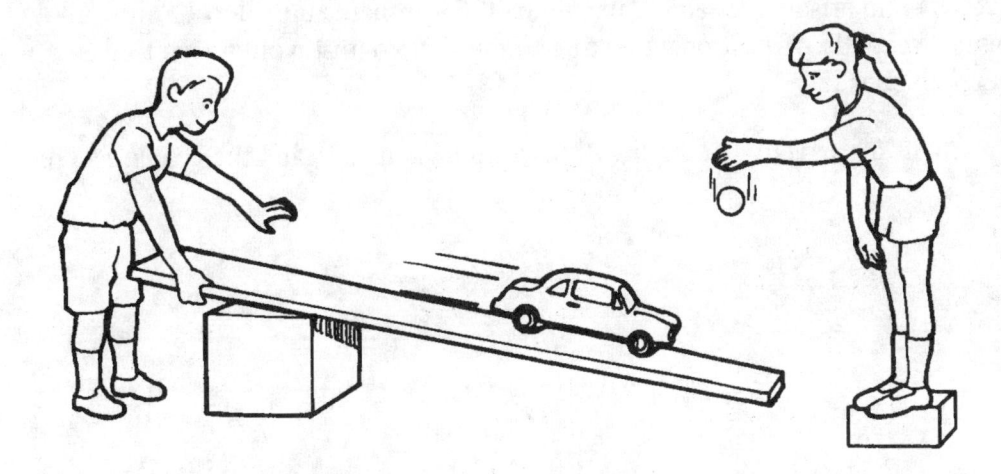

Discussion

The tennis ball represents the *Pathfinder* spacecraft, and the car represents Mars as it moves through space. The students should be able to clearly see that the motion of Mars must be anticipated.

© *Teacher Created Materials, Inc.*

Unmanned Missions to Mars

Activity #14: Time Delay

Have you ever been in a lightning storm? If you have, you know all too well that you see the flash of lightning before you hear the clap of thunder. Or maybe you have watched a fireworks display where the fireworks explode only to be followed a second or two later with a loud BANG! You are experiencing a time delay.

Light travels through the air at a speed of almost 300,000 km per second (186,000 miles per second), but sound travels through the air at a speed of 0.3 km per second (0.2 miles per second—or about 720 miles per hour). And sound travels even slower as you gain altitude. So it is no wonder that you see the lightning before hearing the thunder or that you see the fireworks before hearing the BANG!

Light is the fastest traveling medium we know. And light is a part of the electromagnetic spectrum which includes items such as x-rays, television waves, and radio waves. In order to communicate with the *Pathfinder* lander and the *Sojourner* rover, scientists need to contact them via radio waves.

This poses a bit of a problem. With Mars being between 127–610 million km (79–379 million miles) away from Earth at any given time, there will be some delay in the signal. Let's figure out how long it could take a signal to reach Mars from Earth. This is an illuminating activity for students to try. You may want to pose it as a math exercise.

Shortest Signal Time: 127,000,000 km at 300,000 km/sec = 423 seconds (or 7 minutes)

Longest Signal Time: 610,000,000 km at 300,000 km/sec = 2,033 seconds (or 34 minutes)

Wow! Can you imagine trying to send a signal and not having it get there for over 30 minutes? And what's worse is that the response will take the same amount of time!

Just to give you a comparison, the radio delay when the astronauts talked to Earth from the surface of the moon was 1.3 seconds. An astronaut talking to mission control would have to wait a whole 2.6 seconds to get a response!

On page 69 you will try an activity which will help students understand the problems presented by time delay.

Unmanned Missions to Mars

Activity #14: Time Delay *(cont.)*

Materials
- instructions on page 70
- index cards

Procedure
1. Make a photocopy of the instruction cards on page 70.
2. Cut out the cards and paste them to sturdy index cards.
3. Seat the students on the floor in a circle facing each other.
4. The students should be seated so they are next to each other with the exception of two students who should be separated so that three students could easily be able to sit between them. Essentially, this will give you an "open mouthed" circle on the floor.
5. Give the instruction cards to a student who is seated at the end of the "open mouth." The job of this student is to turn over one of the cards and whisper its instructions into the ear of the person sitting directly next to him or her. In turn that person is to whisper it to the next person until the person on the other end of the "open mouth" does what the instruction says to do.

Discussion
Not only should students notice a delay in their signal, but they might also notice that the student who is supposed to carry out the instructions may not do them correctly. This will be especially true if the instructions are long and require a number of actions. Sometime, messages can break down as they travel to *Pathfinder*, and the *Sojourner* rover may not get clear instructions. The same might happen in this activity!

Unmanned Missions to Mars

Activity #14: Time Delay *(cont.)*

Note: You may want to hold onto the more complicated instructions until the students have had a chance to try this activity a few times.

Stand up and raise your left hand.	Stand up and raise your right hand.
Stand up and turn around three times.	Stand up and turn around one time.
Stand up and jump in place two times.	Stand up and jump in place five times.
Stand up and put one hand on your head and one hand on your stomach. Then jump up and down two times.	Stand up, put both hands on your head, and stand on your left leg.
Stand up, walk three steps forward, and then turn around and jump two times in place. Then, sit down and raise your left hand.	Stand up, walk two steps backward, and then jump three times in place. Then, sit down and raise your right hand.

Unmanned Missions to Mars

Global Surveyor

Surveyor Spacecraft

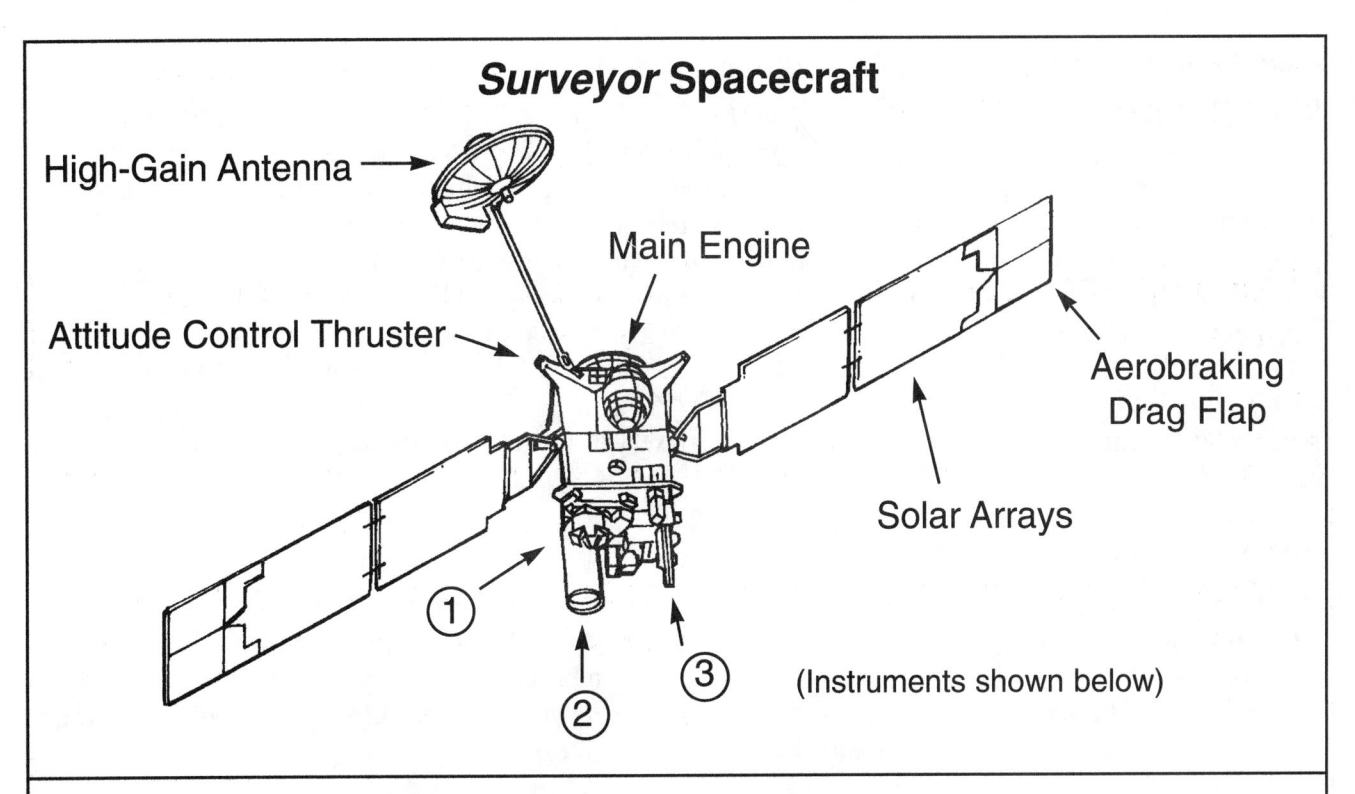

- High-Gain Antenna
- Main Engine
- Attitude Control Thruster
- Aerobraking Drag Flap
- Solar Arrays

① ② ③ (Instruments shown below)

Instruments Aboard Surveyor

① Mars Orbital Laser Altimeter (MOLA)

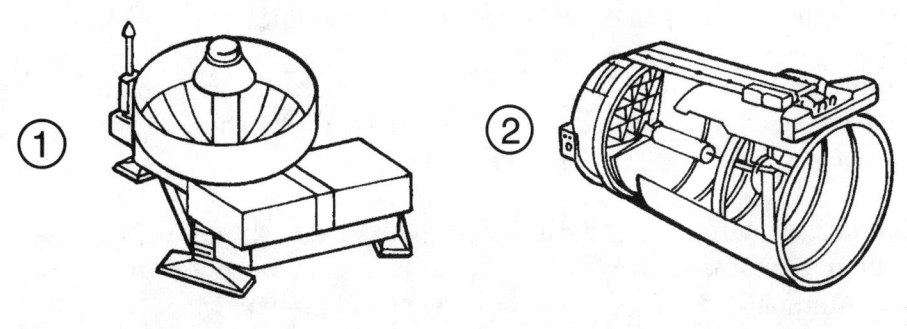

② Mars Orbital Camera (MOC)

③ Mars Relay Radio System (MR)

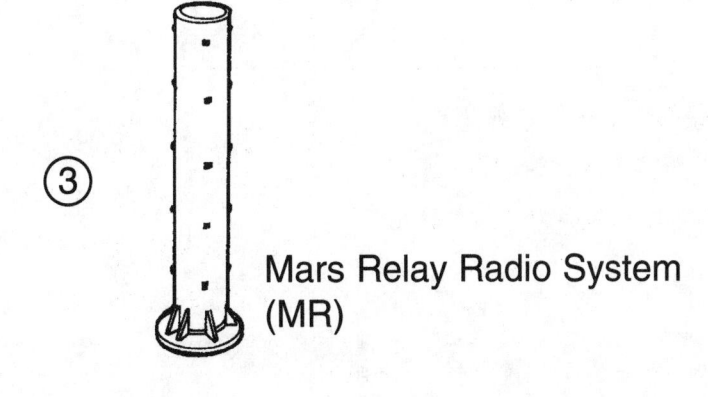

© Teacher Created Materials, Inc. 71 #2383 *Exploring Mars and Beyond—Challenging*

Unmanned Missions to Mars

Global Surveyor (cont.)

Global Surveyor http//mgs-www.jpl.nasa.gov

Like the *Pathfinder*, the *Global Surveyor* is designed to be a part of NASA's new faster, smaller, cheaper series of missions to Mars. Also like *Pathfinder*, the *Global Surveyor* has specific mission objectives which will help build a collective body of knowledge for understanding Mars as well as contribute to the building of future missions to the red planet. Based on information sent back by probes such as *Surveyor* and *Pathfinder*, future space probes under development can be modified.

The mission objective of the *Global Surveyor* is to recover some of the objectives intended for the Mars *Observer* spacecraft which lost contact with Earth on August 21, 1993, before it reached Mars (see page 61 for more information about the Mars *Observer*). As of this writing, *Global Surveyor* has achieved a polar orbit around Mars and is beginning to make observations of the northern and southern polar ice caps of Mars.

Specific Details

Global Surveyor, with a mass of 1,050 kg (2,310 lbs), was launched on November 7, 1996, aboard a Delta II rocket from the Kennedy Space Center, and it reached Mars on September 12, 1997. *Global Surveyor* used the atmosphere of Mars to slow it down in a process known as *aerobraking*. The ultimate goal of this process was to put the *Global Surveyor* in a polar orbit as opposed to an equatorial orbit. A complete polar orbit was finally achieved in January of 1998.

Once in orbit, the *Global Surveyor* used its instruments to map the surface of Mars. These instruments include among other devices, an orbital camera, a laser altimeter, and a Mars relay radio system.

Mars Orbital Camera (MOC): This is the primary camera aboard *Surveyor*. Its purpose is to map the surface of the planet over the course of one Martian year (687 days) to notice surface changes during the Martian seasons. (Mars has seasons like the Earth!)

Mars Orbital Laser Altimeter (MOLA): By sending a laser beam to the surface of Mars and waiting for its reflection to return, the *Global Surveyor* is able to map the topography of the planet. This will be important information for future missions which will land on Mars.

Mars Relay (MR): This instrument allows the *Global Surveyor* to become a communications link for future American, European, and Russian surface landers and rovers. Through this device, those landers can communicate with Earth.

Unmanned Missions to Mars

Activity #15: Capturing the Satellite

Once the *Global Surveyor* made its way to Mars, it next had to be captured by Mars' gravity so it would not just zip past it and fly off into deep space. JPL scientists designed *Global Surveyor* to get close enough to Mars so that the gravity of the planet would slow down the spacecraft and ultimately pull it into a stable orbit.

One of the best methods of explaining how gravity works is by comparing gravity to magnetism. The following activity will help your students understand the nature of gravity. In this case, the magnet will play the role of Mars, and the metal ball bearing will play the role of the *Global Surveyor* spacecraft.

Materials

- rulers
- books
- tape
- metal ball bearings (or magnetic marbles)
- magnets

Procedure

1. Set up the ruler at a ramp. See the drawing below. Be sure to tape the ruler into place.
2. Roll the ball bearing so that it rolls straight off the ruler.
3. Next, position the magnet at the bottom of the ruler so that it is just to the side of the ruler and its magnetic pull will divert the ball bearing from its straight path.
4. Roll the ball bearing and watch its path being diverted by the magnet. Sometimes, the magnet will pull the ball bearing so hard that the ball bearing will stick to the magnet.

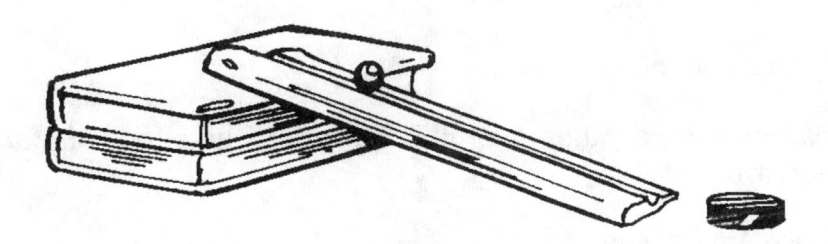

Unmanned Missions to Mars

Future Missions to Mars

What's Next?

With the advent of improving computer technology and tighter budgets from the Federal Government, NASA has had to change the way it does business in space. Computers have advanced to such an extent that the computer you have on your desk at home or at school has far more computer power than was on the *Apollo* missions to the moon! This is good news for NASA because they can now build complex machines with very tiny computers in them. Miniaturization is the key to space travel. The bigger the spacecraft, the more expensive it is to build and put into orbit.

Further, Congress has been slowly reducing the amount of money it spends on space exploration, so scientists at NASA have had to get by on less and less money. The plan for the future includes launching smaller, faster, and cheaper space probes at a more frequent rate than in the past. The hope is that the collective knowledge gathered from these missions will be more productive than sending one massive probe which, if it fails, would doom the entire program.

NASA currently has a 10-year plan to launch one mission every 26 months in 1998, 2001, 2003, and 2005. These missions will be comprised of orbiters, landers, rovers, and probes to Mars.

Future Time Line (Year of Launch)

- **1998: Mars *Surveyor '98* Orbiter**

  Mission is to fly a polar orbit of Mars.

- **1999: Mars *Surveyor '98* Lander**

  Mission is to land near Martian south pole, no rover on board.

- **2001: Mars *Surveyor '01* Orbiter**

  Mission is to analyze mineralogy and chemistry of the planet.

- **2002: Mars *Surveyor '02* Lander**

  Mission is to release a rover on the Martian surface. Rocks will be collected and stored.

- **2003: To Be Announced**

  Mission is for another rover to complement the efforts of *Mars Surveyor '02*.

- **2004: To Be Announced**

  Mission is to pick up the rocks from *Mars Surveyor '02* and return to Earth.

Life on Mars?

Early Views on Life

Ever since Galileo first started looking at the sky with his telescope in 1609, astronomers have been focusing their attention on planets such as Mars. In 1877 the Italian astronomer, Giovanni Schiaparelli, saw a series of straight lines on Mars which he called *channels*. And in 1906 American astronomer Percival Lowell interpreted these channels to be an intricate series of canals carved into the surface of the planet by an intelligent Martian form of life. Ideas that Martians existed were further advanced by Orson Welles' dramatic radio broadcast of H.G. Wells' *War of the Worlds* in 1938. The world had become fascinated with Mars and the possibility of life on the planet.

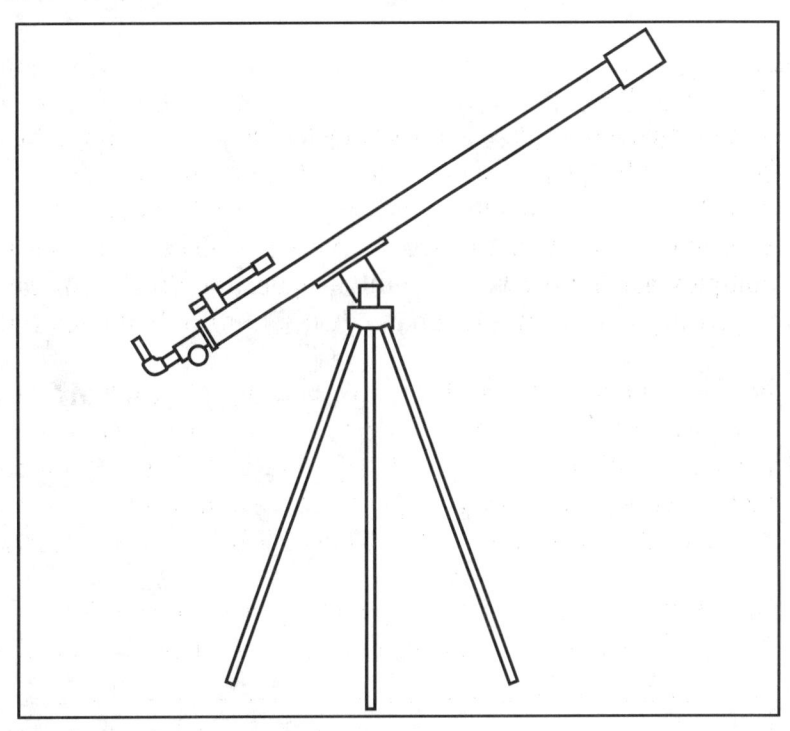

Early Missions to Mars Look for Life

In 1965 *Mariner 4* made the first successful flyby of Mars and found Mars to be a desolate planet with no signs of life. While *Mariner 4* could identify frost on the rims of craters on Mars, it found no signs of life.

In 1976 when the *Viking* landers scooped up the first dirt on Mars and analyzed it, they found no signs of organic material. *Viking* also reconfirmed scientists' understanding of a thin Martian atmosphere dominated by carbon dioxide. Evidence from these missions seems to have all but ruled out the possibility of life on Mars.

Mars Meteorite http://www.jsc.nasa.gov/pao/flash/Marslife/index.html

In 1984, a discovery was made in Antarctica which would ultimately force scientists to re-examine the question "Is there life on Mars?" This discovery was of a meteorite known as ALH84001. Meteorites are discovered frequently since Earth is constantly being bombarded by cosmic dust and debris, but ALH84001 was found to be a special meteorite. In 1993 scientists performing studies on the meteorite found that it contained certain gases and other formations which were strikingly similar to the igneous rocks found on the Martian surface by the *Viking* landers.

The best guess about how it got here is that Mars must have been struck by a large meteorite itself over 3 billion years ago, and that meteorite must have dislodged a large chunk of the planet and sent it off into space. By looking at the sedimentary rock layers in which ALH84001 landed, scientists have determined that the meteorite must have struck Earth some 13,000 years ago.

Life on Mars?

Mars Meteorite

Upon inspection of this meteorite, some scientists believe that they have found evidence of life. Some scientists believe they have found organic molecules and even the fossilized remains of some very simple life forms (such as bacteria or worms). This observation, however, is currently being fiercely debated and argued.

No matter the result of this argument, it is highly unlikely that ALH84001 holds definitive proof that life existed on Mars some 3.6 billion years ago. But just because it doesn't necessarily hold proof that life existed, it doesn't rule it out either.

Mars Meteorite ALH84001

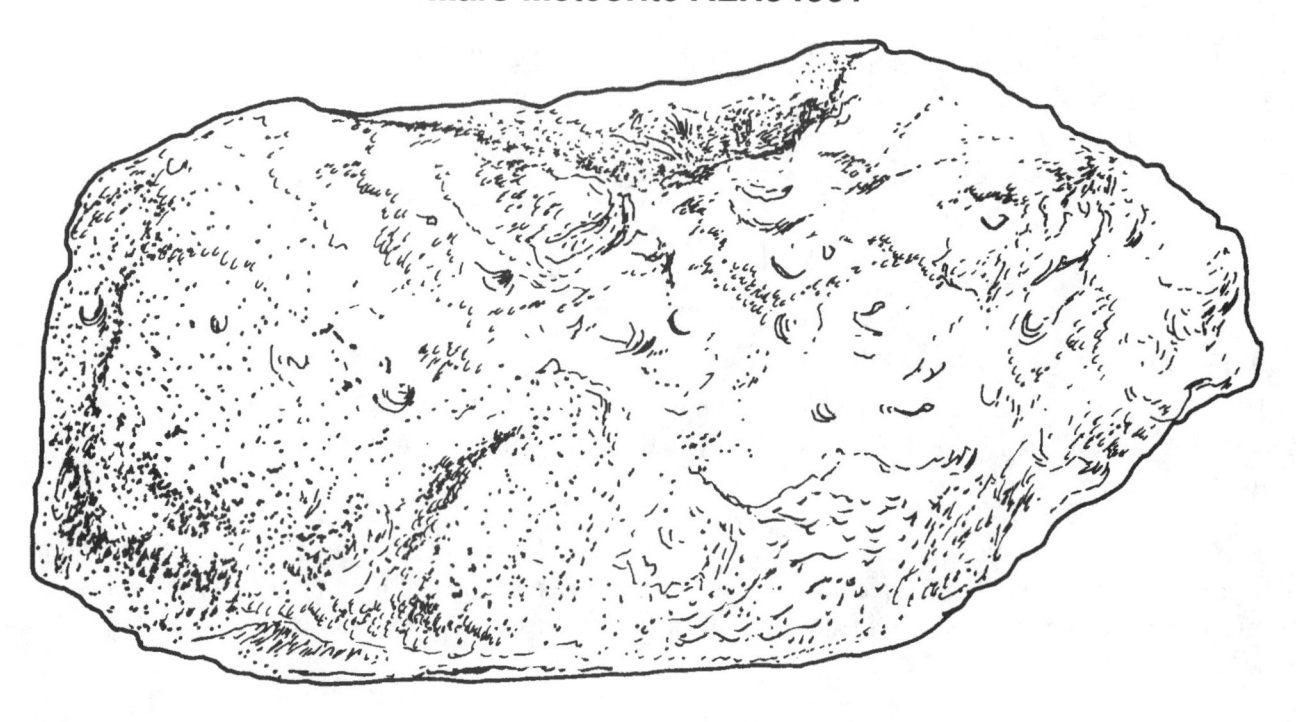

Future Plans for Finding Life

The current missions of the *Pathfinder* and *Global Surveyor* are not intended to search for life on Mars. Their mission objectives are more geological than biological. *Pathfinder* and *Global Surveyor* are intended to study the geology of the planet and determine appropriate landing sites for future missions to Mars.

Remember that NASA's plan for the next 10 years is to send a series of missions to Mars in which each mission will be used as a springboard for future missions. The ultimate goal of these missions is to one day send people to Mars.

Several of the missions planned for Mars include landing craft designed to look for life or the remains of life. But for now, the question remains unanswered and fiercely debated. The scientific and philosophical ramifications of the possibility of life on Mars have continued to intrigue humankind long after people such as Schiaparelli, Lowell, and Wells fantasized about it.

Astronomy and Space Science Report

Now that your students are familiar with the space program and a few basic facts about physics and astronomy, they are ready to complete astronomy and space science reports.

Provide the following list of topics to your students:

Astronomy and Space Science Topics

- History of Rocketry (include Robert Goddard, Wernher von Braun, the V-2, and *Sputnik*)
- Unmanned missions to the moon (*Ranger, Luna, Surveyor, Zond*)
- Unmanned missions to the inner planets until 1980 (*Mars, Mariner, Viking,* etc.)
- Unmanned missions to the inner planets from 1980 on (*Pathfinder, Magellan,* etc.)
- Unmanned missions to the outer planets (*Pioneer, Voyager, Galileo,* etc.)
- Future unmanned missions (*Cassini,* etc.)
- How to become an astronaut (history of famous astronauts and how to become one)
- Manned *Mercury* missions
- Manned *Gemini* missions
- Manned *Vostok* and *Voskhod* missions
- Project *Apollos* #1–11
- Project *Apollos* #12–17
- *Apollo Soyuz* and *STS-71* (U.S. and Soviet joint missions)
- *Skylab* and the "Vomit Comet"
- Space Shuttle
- Space Station *Mir*
- Life on Mars?

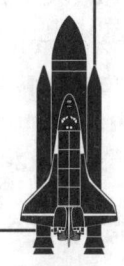

Assign one or two students to be responsible for researching and presenting a topic to the class. They should provide background information on their topic as well as a visual aid. The visual aid should include a time line of events relative to their topic as well as drawings or pictures.

To do their research, students may use the Web pages associated with each topic as well as the books listed in the resources section (see pages 78–80). It is important that each of the topics be covered so that the presentations to the class will form a complete picture of the space program.

Technology Connections

Useful Mars Web Sites

While the following sites do not represent a complete listing of sites dealing with Mars, they collectively cover the information contained within this unit on Mars exploration.

Mars

http://bang.lanl.gov/solarsys/Mars.html
This basic Mars page offers a great deal of information about Mars as well as links to several other sites dealing with Mars and its exploration.

http://currentsky.com/sky_stuff/feb97/feb97.html
An excellent explanation and illustration of retrograde motion appears here.

http://astro/Sun.tn.cornell.edu/Marsnet/mnhome.html
The Mars Net Web site allows you to see where Mars will be in the nighttime sky, a great site if you are planning an evening star party with your students. You can even subscribe to the free *International Mars Watch Electronic Newsletter*.

http://cmex-www.arc.nasa.gov/
Over 65 links to Mars-related information divided into three categories are available at this Center for Mars Exploration (CMEX) site. This award-winning home page is sponsored by NASA's Ames Research Center.

http://www.jsc.nasa.gov/pao/flash/Marslife/index.html
Get the facts about the possibility of life on Mars at this site. This site also contains detailed information about the Martian meteorite, ALH84001.

http://www.reston.com/astro/Mars/catalog.html
This is another site which showcases the life-on-Mars debate. Arguments for and against the possibility of life on Mars are included at this site.

Exploring Mars

http://www.jpl.nasa.gov/
Jet Propulsion Laboratory's home page, this contains a whole section devoted to all unmanned missions launched by JPL.

http://mpfwww.jpl.nasa.gov/
This is Mars *Pathfinder* mission home page.

http://mpfwww.jpl.nasa.gov/rover/descrip.html
Everything you ever wanted to know about the *Sojourner* rover can be found here.

http://mpfwww.jpl.nasa.gov/ops/asimet.html
Want to know the latest weather on Mars? Check out this site.

http://www.lpl.arizona.edu/imp
Learn about the cameras used on *Pathfinder* and see some of the 3-D pictures it has taken.

http:mgs-www.jpl.nasa.gov
This is Mars *Global Surveyor* mission home page.

http://nssdc.gsfc.nasa.gov/planetary
National Space Science Data Center (NSSDC) is NASA's archive for lunar and planetary data and images. At this site you can find out about past missions to the moon, Mars, and other planets as well as find a chronology of lunar and planetary exploration.

http://planetary.org
The Planetary Society promotes the advancement of space exploration and sponsored the contest to name the *Sojourner* rover. Visit this site for their home page.

Technology Connections

Useful Mars Web Sites *(cont.)*

General Astronomy/Space Science Sites

http://www2.ari.net/home/odenwald.cafe.html
At the Astronomy Cafe, you can find the answers to over 3,000 questions asked of Sten Odenwald, a scientist at NASA-Goddard space center. If your question isn't here, send Sten an e-mail.

http://www.sti.nasa.gov/www.html
This site lists links to every single NASA Web site imaginable.

http://www.nss.org/askastro
Ask an Astronaut is a Web page devoted to learning about astronauts. Each month this Web site features a present or former astronaut to answer questions.

http://www.nauts.com
The Astronaut Connection is an award winning page which chronicles man's (and woman's) ventures into space. At this site, you can find a good historical background on many of the manned and unmanned missions into space.

http://shuttle.nasa.gov/sts-74/orbit/mir/mirinfo.html
This site includes pictures and descriptions of the *Mir* space station.

http://space.magnificent.com/human/shuttle&mir
This site includes pictures and descriptions of the *Mir* space station as well as a history of the shuttle missions which have linked up with the Russian space station.

http://www.ksc.nasa.gov
This is the Kennedy Space Center home page, and it includes a wonderful historical section on manned space flight. Be sure to check out the *Mercury*, *Gemini*, and *Apollo* missions at this site.

Collaborative Projects

http://www.stolaf.edu/network/iecc/
A new twist on an old concept! If you visit this Web site, St. Olaf College in Minnesota will set you and your classroom up with another classroom of "e-mail pen pals." You can correspond with students from all over the globe. Perhaps you can ask them to send you a sample of their soil.

http://www.kidlink.org/KIDPROJ/projects.html
Interested in doing a global project? By visiting this site you and your students can collaborate on projects which have global ramifications. Some projects done in the past have included Wetlands, Plate Tectonics, Deserts, and Inventions. You are limited only by your imagination.

Resources

Related Materials and Services

Astronomical Society of the Pacific (ASP): 390 Ashton Ave., San Francisco, CA 94112. (800)335-2624. Request a free catalog showing a wide selection of materials related to astronomy, including slides, posters, videos, and computer software. Teachers are also eligible to receive free copies of *The Universe in the Classroom*, a quarterly newsletter produced by ASP. You will need to request a copy on school letterhead.

Jet Propulsion Laboratory (JPL): Mail Stop CS-530, 4800 Oak Grove Drive, Pasadena, CA 91109. JPL's Teacher Resource Center: (818)354-6916. The Teacher Resource Center offers a selection of free videos, press packets, posters, and CD-ROMs describing the *Pathfinder* and *Global Surveyor* missions.

NASA's Central Operation of Resources for Educators (CORE): Lorain County JVS, 15181 Route 28 South, Oberlin, OH 44074. (216)774-1051 x293. Provides material from NASA to use with students, including slides, videos, and photographs taken from satellites and space missions. Send your request on school letterhead for a free catalog.

National Geographic Society: PO Box 2118, Washington, DC 20013-2118. (800)447-0647. Supplies maps and posters such as The Heavens, The Earth's Moon, Solar System/Celestial Family, and The Universe. Back issues of *National Geographic* may be ordered.

National Science Teachers Association (NSTA): (800)722-6782. Available for purchase through their catalog: books, posters, and CD-ROMs related to astronomy and other sciences. Order a free catalog.

The Planetary Society: 65 North Catalina Ave., Pasadena, CA 91106-9899. (818)793-5100. Co-founded by the late Carl Sagan, the Planetary Society sponsored the naming of the *Sojourner* rover and has an extensive catalog of materials on space exploration.

Related Books, CD-ROMs, and Periodicals

Mars *Navigator*, Georgia Institute of Technology. This interactive, multimedia CD-ROM about Mars and the *Pathfinder* mission is available through JPL. Contact catherine.1.davis@jpl.gov for your free copy while supplies last!

Eyewitnesses Encyclopedia of Space and the Universe, DK Multimedia New York, NY. (800)356-6575. http://www.dk.com. A great deal of information about astronomy and space exploration is contained on this highly interactive disc. If you buy only one science CD-ROM this year, this should be it.

Famighetti, Robert (editor) *The World Almanac 1997*. K-III Reference Co., 1996. When you need a fact, who else are you going to call? It's amazing how many answers are contained within the *Almanac*.

Gallant, Roy A. *Our Universe*. National Geographic, 1994. (800)447-0647. A wonderful picture atlas of the planets and our universe. A must-have reference.

Gardner, Paul. *Internet for Teachers and Parents* (TCM668). Teacher Created Materials, Inc., 1996. (800)662-4321. A fabulous how-to-get-connected-to-the-Internet book. Easy to read and lots of great ideas.

Kluger, Jeffrey. "Uncovering the Secrets of Mars." *Time*, July 14, 1997. Outstanding text, photos, and diagrams from the award-winning science author and journalist.

Neal, Valerie. *Smithsonian Guides: Spaceflight*. Macmillan, 1995. A must-have resource on anything and everything that ever went into space. Fully illustrated.

Sagan, Carl. *Cosmos*. Random House, Inc., NY, 1980. Based on the 13-part television series, this excellent book explains astronomy in layman's terms.

Shepard, Alan and Deke Slayton. *Moon Shot*. Turner Publishing, Inc., 1994. The story of America's race to the moon is told by two of America's original seven astronauts.

Young, Ruth M. *Science Simulations* (TCM2107). Teacher Created Materials, Inc., 1997. (800)662-4321. Simulations include a trip to Mars in the year 2025, as well as communicating with intelligent life beyond our solar system.

Young, Ruth, M. *Space (Intermediate)*. Teacher Created Materials, Inc., 1994. (800)662-4321. This teacher's guide includes hands-on activities related to the solar system, moon, and space travel.